MW00620581

Inviting Him In

Inviting Him In

How the Atonement Can Change Your Family

Wayne E. Brickey

SALT LAKE CITY, UTAH

Visit us at deseretbook.com

Library of Congress Cataloging-in-Publication Data

Brickey, Wayne E.
Inviting Him in : how the atonement can change your family / Wayne E. Brickey.
p. cm.
Includes bibliographical references and index.
ISBN 1-57008-958-2 (alk. paper)
1. Family—Religious life. 2. Church of Jesus Christ of Latter-day Saints—Doctrines.
3. Mormon Church—Doctrines. I. Title.
BX8643.F3B75 2003
248.4—dc21 2003010615

Printed in the United States of America 72076-7076
Publishers Printing, Salt Lake City, UT

10 9 8 7 6 5 4 3 2 1

Through the centuries, many of the sons of Adam and daughters of Eve have done all they could to welcome Jesus Christ into their homes and relationships. Such persons have quietly but dramatically blessed the course of human history. This book is fondly dedicated to their memory.

Contents

Acknowledgments xi
Introduction xiii

Part One: Built on Eternity

1 Answers 3
2 A Home, Not Just a World 6
3 Your Pearl of Great Price 10
4 He Redeems and Saves Families 13
5 The Family Friend 17
6 The Father's Covenant 22
7 A Personal Matter 26
8 Glimpses 30

Part Two: Gathered with Our Fathers

9 "The Offering" 35
10 The Blessings of the Fathers 38
11 Key Moments in History 42
12 A Family That Serves Families 46
13 Gathering: Turning to the Lord 50
14 Scattering: Desolate Dwellings 53

15 Restoring the Eternal 56
16 Glimpses 60

PART THREE: WELDED BY FIRE

17 A Flame from Heaven 65
18 Bigger than We Are 69
19 Staying Together 74
20 Meet for Each Other 79
21 The Lofty Soul of Woman 84
22 The Blessing Role of Man 88
23 Influencing Souls 92
24 Glimpses 95

PART FOUR: JOINED BY CHILDREN

25 Mothers as Angels 103
26 Fathers as "Treasurers" 107
27 The Enormous Life of a Child 111
28 Inviting Your Friends Home 114
29 A Day for Strong Souls 117
30 A Decade for Becoming Strong 121
31 Raising the Strong 126
32 Glimpses 131

PART FIVE: FILLED WITH LIGHT

33 The Grace of Christ 141
34 Grace at Home 146
35 The Madness of Anger 149
36 Eternal Life and Private Life 152
37 Parents Who Teach 156
38 That They May Know of Christ 160
39 Home as a Living Lesson 164
40 Glimpses 167

PART SIX: SURROUNDED BY HOME

41 A House of Order 177
42 The Lord Worketh by Means 181
43 Spiritual Hygiene 185
44 Destiny by Council 189
45 A Covenant of Work 193
46 Getting Things Done 198
47 The Law of Home 202
48 Glimpses 205

PART SEVEN: SEALED TO HEAVEN

49 The Righteous Need Not Fear 213
50 The Friends of God 218
51 Keeping Our "Possessions" 222

52 A Saving Family 227
53 A Saving Covenant 232
54 He Will Not Barge In 236
55 A Kingdom Is Prepared 239
56 Glimpses 244
Index 249

Acknowledgments

I suppose this book would be perfect if it depended only on my wife, Joanne. Thanks to her support, I was able to work under the best of circumstances. I am also indebted to one of our sons, Joseph Brickey, whose art appears on the cover and at the beginning of each part of this book. Nor have Joseph and Karen Watkins, Michael Morris, Richard Erickson, Tonya Facemyer, Kathie Terry, and Cory Maxwell left me with any excuse. However, gracious friends can compensate for an author only so much. To the extent that this book falls short, I alone must accept the responsibility.

Introduction

Why is the family so essential? What is its destiny? How can an imperfect family receive divine help in reaching its eternal potential?

Those questions repeatedly beckon us to the words of the prophets, who present us with a goal—the perfected family. Our bridge to that goal is Christ, who vows to be a part of every home that invites him in. He is not discouraged with the great distance most of us have to travel to reach the ideal. If we will be faithful, he will get us there, and we will partake of his fulness. Through him, the ailing can be healed, and the ideal can become real.

This book examines some of the principles that invite the Savior's quiet heavenly power into our loud down-to-earth homes. Its chapters are small, gathered into seven sections, or parts. At the close of each part, I have included a chapter called "Glimpses," aimed at illustrating principles.

To the extent that you find this book helpful, I am very grateful. It will be one more evidence that we are not alone.

Built on Eternity

We never have to apologize for our belief in marriage and family, no matter how inconvenient or awkward it seems in this rather unheavenly world we live in, and no matter how deficient our own life seems to be. The pure patterns of marriage and family come directly from the eternal worlds. Heaven itself is the family blueprint, and the expert Creator helps us build (Matthew 7:24–25; D&C 33:12–13). Through the Father's Son, the Rock foundation, we build with perfect plans on perfect footings.

> *I am Messiah, the King of Zion, the Rock of Heaven, which is broad as eternity* (Moses 7:53).

The chapters and glimpses in Part One examine the great program of family salvation. The heavenly ideal may seem a far cry from where we are living right now, which is a good reason to think about the plan we once agreed upon. If we want to return home, we need to repeatedly look at that plan.

Chapter 1

ANSWERS

Behold, I stand at the door, and knock: if any man hear my voice, and open the door, I will come in to him (Revelation 3:20).

At the entrance of many modest homes throughout the world today, a drape or veil, instead of a wooden slab, covers the doorway. So it was with the poor of ancient Israel. A visitor would knock on the outside of the opening, and the host would respond by parting the curtain and offering a welcome. It was a welcome with open arms.

It is at the door of a home—yours or mine, for example—that Jesus knocks. He knocks because he would sincerely like to enter and be a part of our family life. He would like to counsel and befriend us, participate in our decisions, soften our hearts, heal us, and reform us. He has great plans for your family and mine—even if we don't seem to have a family right now.

As we will see in the coming pages, what he has in mind for us is perfection. We might feel discouraged if we compare that goal with our situation at home. After all, most of us fall short somewhere, and many of us are so far from his ideal that we can hardly picture it. But in this book, we will try to picture it anyway. Our purpose is to trust the ideal and to realize that, with Christ's help, we can attain it in due time.

The reason we fall short might be that we inherited someone else's mistake. Or maybe our problem goes back to a time when we were foolish or faithless. In any case, we are where we are, and we cannot change the past.

The question that should tear at our hearts now deals with the future. Can we who are imperfect, or who seem so entirely chained to unhappy situations, ever have a complete and happy family? The gospel answer is a decisive "Yes!" All of the faithful, no matter what their past may be, can have a fulness of family joy.

As the Redeemer, Christ can overrule the past. As the Savior, he can enter into our present as a friend might enter a modest and careworn household, first mending one thing and then another. He can carry us, change after change, into a perfect future. That is what he promises. And his greatest promises are family promises. Our Personal Friend is also our Family Friend. However, this Friend is a gentleman. He does not enter without invitation.

Just how do we bid the living Christ to join us? We offer our invitation by offering ourselves, in a covenant. Of our own free will, we enter into the gospel agreement. Then we confirm that invitation day in and day out by being true to what we said we would do for him. This is our unmistakable language of love, our means of asking for his healing and sealing presence in our home.

Imagine the burden Adam and Eve must have felt when the long, arduous story of humanity—with all its dreadful twists of inhumanity—was just getting underway. From their little beginnings, their first homestead outside the Garden of Eden, would come all the hosts of humankind, all the ways of nations. They surely sensed the emerging, complex succession of lives and histories. They knew that the fallen condition would take its toll, that evil would take some of their posterity by storm, that strife and sorrow would surpass all imagination. How did they dare go forward? And, for that matter, how do we?

Adam and Eve began their mission on their knees, and on their knees they frequently renewed it. From an altar of sacrifice and covenant making, their prayers rose heavenward like a sacred and fragrant cloud. The altar was their sign of obedience, of promise keeping, of remembrance (Moses 5:7–8). The timeless image of a couple at an altar, offering everything so that the living Christ might join them to each other and then join with them at home, holds as much meaning today as it ever has.

After the advent of Christ, mankind was given somewhat different ways of remembering the covenant, and yet it is the same covenant and the same invitation—made with and offered by the same Family Friend. We long for his help just as Adam and Eve did.

The marvelous thing is that our Friend is real, his invitation is real, and his help is real. His Father's program, which this book explores, really does change people. The glorious picture of family salvation is meant for all of us no matter how lost or lonely we think we are. The unfriendly challenges and realities that surround us do not have to stand in the Savior's way. He will resolve or replace them far more easily than we can imagine. So let us not fear. Let us, in faith, answer his knock and let him carry out his plans for our families.

When we have admitted him into our imperfect homes, when he has completed his patient work there, when we at last have families fashioned after his will, what happens then? In a way, we trade places. We approach the entrance to his abode. When he parts the curtain, we will hear his invitation to bring our families—saved by him—into his perfect home.

Well done, thou good and faithful servant: thou hast been faithful over a few things, I will make thee ruler over many things: enter thou into the joy of thy lord (Matthew 25:21; D&C 88:56, 58, 60).

Chapter 2

A Home, Not Just a World

Family was the original source of every soul. Even when the curtain of amnesia is drawn across our premortal family ties, we are immediately immersed in new lineages and profuse relationships. Later, no matter what our kingdom of glory, those who surround us will be none other than brothers and sisters. Family never goes away. It is the great dependable constant.

> *All men and women are in the similitude of the universal Father and Mother, and are literally the sons and daughters of Deity (The First Presidency).*[1]

Before any of us were born as spirit children, there were Parents—personal and perfect. This Mother and Father were covenant beings, bound to you and me by their loving pledge, determination, and pure integrity. They were full of insight, might, and kindness. They were our very own parents, our first reality, and they will always be there. What came first will never end. The original ties cannot be severed.

> *Man, as a spirit, was begotten and born of heavenly parents, and reared to maturity in the eternal mansions of the Father (The First Presidency).*[2]

The heaven of our origin was not just a world. It was a home. Whatever else our heavenly life was, it was family life—happy, stable, and splendid. We had plenty of siblings, of course, but did too many children live there?

Not at all. The Eternal Mother and Father cared for each child fondly, thoroughly.

As we matured there, so did our family reflexes. Affection for our Parents soared into worship. We became more active as citizens in our heavenly home. We polished a thousand talents. Our kinship with family members branched out into friendships that would last forever. But ahead of us lay yet another realm of growth.

> *Our Father has passed through these ordeals, and has trodden the paths we are treading. He kept his second estate, and has attained to his exaltation. We have the privilege of following in his footsteps (Daniel H. Wells).*[3]

When the time came for us to explore beyond our settled premortal ties, a grand and well-laid plan was prepared to guide us to a fulness of family experience. New roles would bring new kinds of love and service, new adventures and duties, new wisdom and capacity. The rewards would surpass anything we had known before.

> *The great plan of happiness (see Alma 42:8, 16) revealed to prophets is the plan for a happy family. It is the love story between husband and wife, parents and children, that renews itself through the ages (Boyd K. Packer).*[4]

If we do not see the love story awaiting each person, couple, and family, we do not understand the plan.

Like our Parents in heaven, we are to have marriages of our own. We were not to remain forever in the cozy but narrow experience of childhood. In making two separate lives into one life, we experience an expanding and demanding joy. In marriage, those who were once spirit siblings become considerably more—mortal spouses. Together, these two beings enter glorious and unfamiliar territory. Never in the eternal past had they experienced anything like marriage.

Going from sibling to spouse is a giant leap in family privileges. Marriage leads to another godlike career: parenthood. Like our Heavenly Parents, we create, nurture, and save other beings. Each of them is new and unique, worth everything to us, as if each were an only child. They also progress, and the love story "renews itself through the ages."

> *Our theology begins with heavenly parents. Our highest aspiration is to be like them (Dallin H. Oaks).*[5]

Our origin gives rise to our goal. We leave Father and Mother that we may learn their way and obtain their nature. We are not simply to return but to return at another level. We leave as children of Deity and come back as replicas of Deity.

Thus, in a message to fathers, the Quorum of the Twelve Apostles said:

> *Fatherhood, in a sense, is an apprenticeship to godhood. . . . The title* father *is sacred and eternal (The Quorum of the Twelve Apostles).*[6]

Stage by stage, the Father's plan changes our relationships with more and more of his children: from premortal sister to eternal wife, daughter, or daughter-in-law; from premortal brother to eternal grandson, uncle, or grandfather; from premortal sibling to eternal ancestor or descendant. Simple links are replaced by endless depth and variety.

> *The family is the great plan of life as conceived and organized by our Father in Heaven (Spencer W. Kimball).*[7]

Obviously, most of us will not proceed directly from that ideal past family to an ideal future family by a short, direct route. We may have little family detours on the way. We may even get turned around at times, needing to refer again and again to the Father's original plan, which acts as a big map for the lost. We may need repairs, and we may experience fender-benders or worse. But none of this should discourage us in the slightest. A system is in place for handling these delays. We must remember that the setbacks are only temporary, that the delays are only lessons, and that we are never alone. Let us look again at the map and go forward with faith.

Notes

1. In *Messages of the First Presidency of The Church of Jesus Christ of Latter-day Saints,* comp. James R. Clark, 6 vols. (Salt Lake City: Bookcraft, 1965–75), 4:203.
2. Ibid., 5:244.
3. *Journal of Discourses,* 26 vols. (London: Latter-day Saints' Book Depot, 1854–86), 16:127.
4. "The Shield of Faith," *Ensign,* May 1995, 9.
5. "Apostasy and Restoration," *Ensign,* May 1995, 8.
6. "Father, Consider Your Ways," *Ensign,* June 2002, 12.
7. *The Teachings of Spencer W. Kimball,* ed. Edward L. Kimball (Salt Lake City: Bookcraft, 1982), 324.

Chapter 3

YOUR PEARL OF GREAT PRICE

The plan of happiness is not about salvation in general but about family salvation in particular—the healing and sealing and saving of families. Once we understand what the prophets have taught us, we can understand our deepest impulses.

> *If there were nothing else given to the world by the Prophet Joseph Smith than our great and beautiful conception of home and family, he would have made the greatest contribution ever made to humanity by any man who has lived (Stephen L Richards).*[1]

Blessed are those who know the real aim of our Father's work. The family is his reason for programs and commandments and meetings and great labors far and wide. In 1831, when the Lord sent some of his people to Missouri—"the land upon which the Zion of God shall stand" (D&C 58:7)—he added this imperative:

> *Let them bring their families to this land (D&C 58:25).*

Despite the hardship and time it took to move so many people and belongings, there would have been no Zion without spouses and parents and children. A community of lonely males does not even remotely fit the great plan. It would be no Zion at all!

The eternal family is the essence, the pearl. Like an astute merchant always on the watch for something precious, the Church is ready to give its all for this treasure (Matthew 13:45–46).

> *The chapel, the stake house, and the temple are sacred as they contribute to the building of the most sacred institution in the Church—the home—and to the blessing of the most sacred relationships in the Church, the family (Boyd K. Packer).*[2]

Once we see where the Father's heart is, we know where to place our own hearts. We can then follow the mysterious story going on right before our eyes. The prophets understand the drama. They know which things are big and which are small. The Church has it right about the family. But the family needs to get it right also. We have to value our pearl in order to possess it. By contrast, the world—isolated from heaven past and heaven future—rarely seeks and little resembles the eternal homestead from which it sprang.

> *The Church itself, with all its saving graces and powers, is in effect a service organization for the family, because exaltation and eternal life (they are synonymous terms) grow out of the continuation of the family unit in eternity (Bruce R. McConkie).*[3]

In the world, we face the danger of growing careless about our pearl. Any interest that would weaken the relationships of heaven past or heaven future cannot meet the test of joy. Maverick connections have no future.

The endless ages to come will never present a crossroad quite like the one before us now. We are deciding whether the fulfillment of family will be ours forever.

How loyal will we be to our origins? How faithful will we be to the

Head of our premortal family? How far will we go to live family principles while in this world between heavens? Will we choose, when the opportunity arrives, to permanently combine our life with the life of another? Will the two of us learn to do this sharing in a graceful and cheerful way? Will we accept the gift of parenthood? Will we be patient with children through thick and thin? Will we fill our family roles even when they seem hard or pointless?

We may not have parents or family of any kind just now. Perhaps we are among those folks who have no one. Nevertheless, there persists in each of us a memory of the ancient family melody. Deep within, we have good answers for eternal questions.

> *His plan for redeeming His children . . . is the* why *of all that God does! (Neal A. Maxwell).*[4]

His plan needs to be the why of all we do. The fulness of family is somewhere on reserve for you and me. It is our pearl of great price—a pearl that is worth giving our all that we might obtain it.

Notes

1. In Conference Reports of The Church of Jesus Christ of Latter-day Saints (Salt Lake City: The Church of Jesus Christ of Latter-day Saints, October 1926), 26.
2. *"That All May Be Edified"* (Salt Lake City: Bookcraft, 1982), 234–35.
3. "The New and Everlasting Covenant of Marriage," *Brigham Young University Speeches of the Year,* 20 April 1960), 4.
4. "Encircled in the Arms of His Love," *Ensign,* November 2002, 16.

Chapter 4

He Redeems and Saves Families

The Father's plan is to transform siblings of spirit into leaders of resurrected families, good children into godly giants. But real growth, the irreversible kind we see in nature, is slow and cellular. It is not always graceful. Not every step is forward. There are blunders, traumas, and breathless near-death moments. Transformation can leave quite a mess.

No growth could occur without the Sponsor. He envisions the outcome, understands every step, champions each individual, and supports a thousand tiny events each moment (Mosiah 2:21). The Sponsor meets the expenses a growing organism could never pay. And the Sponsor cleans up the mess.

He must be a redeeming Sponsor—salvaging, washing, and making up for all the costs of growth (Mosiah 15:12; Alma 5:21; 33:22). To *redeem* means to pay off the bills of others, to bail them out, to rescue them from grim bondage or debt. Every imperfect, indebted family needs the same benefactor: Christ the Redeemer.

Newborns to this earth have just left the magnificent celestial Mother and Father and entered into somewhat darker places and the much weaker arms of a mortal mom and dad, who are learning parenthood and all else. How much of this contrast babies are aware of is not clear, but we wonder if that is what all the crying is about.

We cannot measure what it means for Jesus to redeem a family from angry offenses, injured ties, betrayed laws, forgotten gifts. For the mortal mother or father, the debt of deficiency weighs too much. It etches the memory; it presses and smothers. It has driven strong men, trying to bear it alone, to insanity. It has soured and hardened women who were once gracious.

Jesus the Redeemer knelt before a towering justice to answer it all. Beneath the crushing demands, he absorbed and paid. The exceeding cost of imperfection has been covered. Through him, we may be released from all past sorrows and debts. Even late in life, we may begin to pursue our Father's dream for us.

Those who are redeemed also need to be saved—that is, healed and mended. It would not be enough to have our debts cleared one day if the next day we were just as prone to sink ourselves into new debts. Our bills need to be fixed, but so do we. Our families need Christ the Savior.

> *All flesh shall know that I, the Lord, am thy Savior and thy Redeemer, the Mighty One of Jacob (1 Nephi 21:26).*

When he calls himself our Savior *and* our Redeemer, he is not repeating himself. Wordiness is not in his nature (Ecclesiastes 5:2, 3, 7; Matthew 6:7). Though these two titles overlap, they have two separate meanings. As the redeeming Sponsor, Jesus paid for the right to bless us. As the saving Sponsor, he bestows the blessing. As the Redeemer, he is the wayfaring friend who pays for our stay. As the Savior, he is the innkeeper who nurses us to health (Luke 10:35). The two services are so connected that both must be carried out by the same Servant: personal and family redemption, personal and family salvation.

We can no more save ourselves by our small strength than we can redeem ourselves on our small budget. Consider a minor example: healing a child's earache—excruciating to the little one, agonizing to the onlooking parent. Paying for medical care and giving emotional support can be taxing. What, then, about the price of making a heartache go away? Without a Savior at our side, how could we minister to defects, nourish wounds, foster virtues, or connect separate hearts?

An individual is too complex and delicate to be perfected by the faint therapeutic powers of man. So what about a family full of individuals—not to mention a lineage full of families? It is a project for the Lord Almighty. He is the Redeemer we need to wash us and the Savior we need to anoint us.

Salvation is a vast business. The Savior starts with a person of faith here, and while grooming and polishing that individual he undertakes the same process with someone over there. The two lives then progress along parallel roads, but before they reach their full dimension, the Savior slows the project in order to marry them into one life. The combination of two complex beings does not result in anything very easy or casual, but God sees the project through from individual salvation to marital salvation and from family salvation to lineal salvation. If we let him, he will finish what he starts.

> *All the kindreds of the earth cannot be blessed unless he shall make bare his arm in the eyes of the nations (1 Nephi 22:10).*

It is not only the people of the earth but also the kindreds—the families—that need his help. Thinking he is only interested in certain families tells us a lot about us but nothing about him. No, he has gone to work for *all*—all the families of the earth. That is his project, his covenant, his historic promise, his work and glory (1 Nephi 22:11; Moses 1:39).

When he finally gets around to us, bestowing upon our specific families the customized gifts and treasures of eternal life, there will be only one conclusion to draw: he really is the perfect Redeemer and Savior. If we keep ourselves in his hands, his promises will be our fortune.

> *They shall be brought out of obscurity and out of darkness; and they shall know that the Lord is their Savior and their Redeemer, the Mighty One of Israel (1 Nephi 22:12).*

Chapter 5

The Family Friend

Just as we could not have created ourselves, we are not very self-sustaining once we are created. We lack the keys to our emotional jails. We cannot roll back the stone of death. We have no idea how to build even a one-person heaven for ourselves. Jesus must prepare the mansion, and he alone can prepare a family to live in it. He is the ultimate Family Friend (D&C 81:6; John 14:2, Ether 12:34; and D&C 98:18).

Matthew tells of a young man whose body and spirit were "sore vexed." A father, surely acting in behalf of himself and his wife, came begging Jesus to help (Matthew 17:14–19). We imagine that the parents had their own problems that they might have presented to Jesus, but one matter alone dominated their minds. They had committed their lives to a spirit-sibling who was now their son.

Pleased with their unreserved devotion and responding to their innocent faith, Jesus took their number one problem into his own hands. They had invited their Divine Friend into the family, and he accepted the invitation. First, he rebuked the devil. Perhaps the son had, by some previous choice, submitted himself to Satan's influence. Regardless, Jesus the Redeemer has the buying power to snatch a soul from Satan's grasp whenever he sees fit. He chose this moment to redeem (Mosiah 3:6). Second, he cured the boy. Jesus the Savior made a mighty change.

Whatever Jesus lays his hands upon lives. If Jesus lays his hands upon a marriage, it lives. If he is allowed to lay his hands on the family, it lives (Howard W. Hunter).[1]

Christ's mission, in the service of the Father's plan, is to be the family's closest friend.

The family also has an enemy. He who once opposed the Father's plan now opposes it more than ever. He knows that the plan is all about salvation and family. The Destroyer knows what he wants to destroy.

The single purpose of Lucifer is to oppose the great plan of happiness, to corrupt the purest, most beautiful and appealing experiences of life: romance, love, marriage, and parenthood (Boyd K. Packer).[2]

No wonder it seems that war rages all around the family; Satan's war is all about the family. He wants us shackled to him, not sealed to each other. He has invented all sorts of enticements to persuade our loved ones to put on his iron yoke. To undo those shackles, we must reach for a special hand, strong and stretched out far.

Then shall his yoke depart from off them, and his burden depart from off their shoulders. This is the purpose that is purposed upon the whole earth; and this is the hand that is stretched out upon all nations (2 Nephi 24:25–26; Isaiah 14:26–27).

Earth's story seems to favor the Destroyer, and billions of homes appear to be doomed. But the master plot will yet unfold. God's purpose "upon the whole earth" will turn the grim tides of history. Deliverance is his mission, arising from his very nature. It is what he does. He oversees every story; he monitors every crisis. Those who cannot help themselves will find him there when the right moment comes, turning things around.

Because of the Atonement of the Savior, the plan of happiness will succeed and Satan's plan is doomed to failure (Richard G. Scott).[3]

The Family Friend offers, as a symbol of his perfect friendship, his robe, the *kafar* of ancient Near East tradition. This large and roomy outer garment was used in marriage ceremonies to envelop both husband and wife. It signified their inseparability. The couple used the *kafar* again with the birth of each child. Donning the robe together, the parents would take the baby in with them as a sign of the baby coming under their care and being a full heir to all they would ever have.

Related to this is another use of the *kafar:* the adoption of a needy friend or stranger who comes on bended knee, asking for entrance into the clan. If the leader decides to make the newcomer a fully privileged family member, he stretches forth his arms and opens his robe like the gates of grace. The new adoptee enters the embrace, a solemn covenant is made, and everyone rejoices. There is no second-class citizenship, no such thing as a partial adoption (2 Nephi 4:33–35).

He hath clothed me with the garments of salvation, he hath covered me with the robe of righteousness (Isaiah 61:10).

Tied to the Hebrew word *kafar* is the Hebrew word *kippur*—to cover, protect, carry, join, combine forces with, pay for, rescue. (The English word *cover,* given its spelling and pronunciation, seems to be related to *kafar*). As King James translators encountered *kippur* in the ancient text, they found no English word to equal all of its meanings, so they decided to invent a special word: atone (at + one). (See Exodus 29:33–37; Exodus 30:15; Leviticus 1:4; 10:17; 16:10; Numbers 8:21; 25:13; Nehemiah 10:33). *Atone* was originally pronounced as it appeared: "at one."

Jesus openly offers us the security of his robe of fellowship. In quiet gospel ceremonies, we accept his invitation through covenant and are joined to him in a loyal and lasting relationship. The Atonement joins us with him under its special cover, and it broadens even further in due time, sealing us to each other.

In a way, then, the At-one-ment is not just a payment made in the Holy Land two thousand years ago. It is an active embrace offered by Christ.

Bring forth the best robe, and put it on him (Luke 15:22).

Without Jesus, there would be no Family Friend to envelop husband and wife, parent and child, in the best robe. With him, there are plenty of robes to go around for all the returning children.

And white robes were given unto every one of them (Revelation 6:11; 7:9).

Considering how central the family is to Jesus and how central he is to the family, we might think of the Second Coming as a family event, a triumphant reunion, where the family will gather to its Sponsor. But to prepare for this sacred reception, parents and children must turn to each other, or else "the whole earth would be utterly wasted at his coming" (D&C 2:3; Malachi 4:6).

Many hearts—more than we might imagine—will be turned. Though no one will be forced, multitudes of families will attend. Jesus once gave this preview to our ancestor Enoch:

> *Then shalt thou and all thy city meet them there, and we will receive them into our bosom, and they shall see us, and we will fall upon their necks, and they shall fall upon our necks, and we will kiss each other (Moses 7:63).*

Those who abide that day will see two wondrous realities combined as one, like two hands fitting into one perfect clasp: the family as one hand, the living Christ as the other. Before us will stand the Son of God, whom we will worship. Around us will be the loved ones he has saved and sealed. That will be a day of embraces. It will commence an endless stream of affections.

> *I shall come in my glory in the clouds of heaven, to fulfil the promises that I have made unto your fathers (D&C 45:16).*

Notes

1. "Reading the Scriptures," *Ensign,* November 1979, 65.
2. "For Time and All Eternity," *Ensign,* November 1993, 21.
3. "Finding Happiness," *Brigham Young University 1996–97 Speeches* (Provo, Utah: Brigham Young University Publications, 1997), 364.

Chapter 6

THE FATHER'S COVENANT

At the center of the gospel are two announcements, two items of good news excelling all other headlines in history.

First is the Father's offer to form us into celestial families. By itself, that offer is stunning but daunting. It offers galactic crowns but requires universal law. It is a rising path. We novices, fresh out of heaven, would not get far on that path all by ourselves.

Fortunately, the second announcement makes the rigorous realistic: we are not alone on the path. The Atonement, the Son's offering, complements the Father's offering. It helps us along in the plan—to be forgiven of wanderings, recover from fatigues, and move to new levels. These offerings are not just ideas; they have actually been delivered.

Along with the plan and the Atonement, the gospel describes another offering, the one we are to give. Our share, our gift, our offering, is our covenant. The Father and the Son have made their offerings by covenant with us and our ancestors. We receive their offerings by covenants of our own.

> *My soul delighteth in the covenants of the Lord which he hath made to our fathers; yea, my soul delighteth in his grace, and in his justice, and power, and mercy in the great and eternal plan (2 Nephi 11:5).*

Our experiences in the Church are threaded together by covenants, which are gestures of friendship with Christ. By covenants, we exchange gifts with him.

The word *covenant* is used hundreds of times in scripture. It is related to the word *convene*—to meet together, gather, unite, connect, join forces, get acquainted. A covenant is much more than a contract. With a covenant, there is no careful inspection of fine print, no rushing for advantage, no guarded meeting, no wary signing. It is the joining of hearts.

> *For this is the covenant that I will make with the house of Israel after those days, saith the Lord; I will put my laws into their mind, and write them in their hearts (Hebrews 8:10).*

He welcomes; we trust. When we try to comprehend our part in the covenant, we discover that giving our all puts us in the close inner circle of the Lord's friends. The covenant becomes sweet to our taste. At length, we welcome him; at last, he can trust us.

Once bound in this way to a living, infinite Being, we never need to be aimless, unattached, unemployed, or unattended again. In this arrangement for mutual giving, what is his part?

> *Eye hath not seen, nor ear heard, neither have entered into the heart of man, the things which God hath prepared for them that love him (1 Corinthians 2:9; D&C 133:45).*

Only in returning to him will we ever fathom what sort of Father he really is and what treasures he has to share. But we do know that his infinite part unfolds in answer to our finite part. We know that granting more and more is just what he wants to do.

I will prove you in all things, whether you will abide in my covenant (D&C 98:14).

The Lord sometimes speaks as if there were just one grand covenant instead of a series of covenants (Genesis 9:9; Ezekiel 20:37; Daniel 9:4; Malachi 3:1; 1 Nephi 15:18; 3 Nephi 15:8; D&C 39:11; 66:2). We may compare his covenant to a puzzle being assembled piece by piece, ordinance by ordinance. Each piece is beautiful in its own right—a small picture. But the ultimate beauty, the whole picture, comes only when the last piece—the highest ordinance—is in place.

After baptism, we make our decision more sure with each added ordinance—like putting more logs on a fire. The picture grows bigger, our commitment warmer. And yet, our covenant remains the same bond of loyalty we promised at the outset. The wholeness of the covenant reminds us of the oneness of gospel law.

For whosoever shall keep the whole law, and yet offend in one point, he is guilty of all (James 2:10).

Behold, I am the law (3 Nephi 15:9).

The gospel is not a list of separate laws. It is one because godliness is seamless. It is one because he is the law, and he is one (3 Nephi 18:24; 27:21, 27).

"The covenant" is like "the law" in this way. Its fulness is whole, a complete bond with our Father. Each successive pledge ties us to him in some added way. Each promise to put him first is, once again, putting him first.

Blessed are you for receiving mine everlasting covenant, even the fulness of my gospel (D&C 66:2).

For example, suppose that some years ago you realized that baptism obligated you to "bear one another's burdens, that they may be light" (Mosiah 18:8). Over time, during the weekly sacrament, you have sometimes thought seriously about this role among your fellow beings. But more recently you have married, and it occurs to you that this burden-sharing business has taken on new meaning! A baptismal promise integrates with the marriage promise. The two covenants blend into something bigger and more celestial than either could have been if kept separate in the mind. In this and a hundred other combinations, the standards and laws of the covenants combine with each other, becoming "the covenant."

Chapter 7

A Personal Matter

To welcome the home teachers, you merely open the door; they will not stay long. To attend a meeting, you just walk in; it will be over in a while. But our covenant making is a long-range commitment. Inviting Christ into the home is no casual matter (2 Kings 23:3).

So an altar—a covenant-making place—is no casual location. The sacrament table of a chapel fits this description. Each week at that modest altar, the Lord presents the symbols of his offering to us while we offer ourselves to him. We are not surprised to find altars in the temple, a perfect meeting spot for the three gospel offerings: the Father's, the Son's, and ours—the plan, the Atonement, the covenant. Christ and the family meet over an altar in the house of the Lord. Promises are exchanged like tender gifts.

What we profess in making promises, we prove by keeping them. Fidelity—doing what we say we will do—is the language of love. It is intensely personal, for only an individual can make a vow. And when inconvenience or pain arises, the decision to honor that vow can be made only in the privacy of a heart. Keeping a trust is a very private matter. A maxim often quoted by Church leaders says, "It is more important to be trusted than to be loved" (Marvin J. Ashton).[1]

The covenant is a personal matter on the Father's part as well. Surely it was so when he made his original proposal to begin with. In a personal way he accepts the hourly gifts we make to him. And what could be more personal than the way in which he will fulfill his promise? (Leviticus 26:9, 11–12).

We are on earth to keep promises. Integrity makes a solid soul and glues us to each other. In great stories, unbending fidelity tips us off to the real hero, the genuine king or queen. Loyalty is royalty.

If a man vow a vow unto the Lord, or swear an oath to bind his soul with a bond; he shall not break his word, he shall do according to all that proceedeth out of his mouth (Numbers 30:1–2; D&C 82:10).

How shall we know our Father's heart? There is no better way than to do according to our vows, to be true to our word, to imitate him "who keepest covenant and mercy" (Nehemiah 9:32; 27–31; 1 Kings 8:56; D&C 98:3). We may have difficulty detecting his love in the occasional stern action he must take as the upholder of all things and defender of all law. But this is simply the greater proof that we can depend upon him.

The mountains shall depart and the hills be removed, but my kindness shall not depart from thee, neither shall the covenant of my peace be removed (3 Nephi 22:10; 22:1–9).

We find him unpredictable in a thousand ways because of the infinitude of his knowledge, the blinding rapidity of his thought, and the staggering innovation and beauty of his handiwork. But one thing about him is entirely knowable: he keeps his word. To subtract his covenant nature from our understanding of him is to downsize and demean him—a switching of gods. He has never been untrue and never will in all the eons that lie ahead.

[God] will never desert us. . . . He cannot do it (George Q. Cannon).[2]

Daily life does not give much priority to our greatest treasure—the connection we have with God. Staring too much at the world, losing focus, we may forget or even forsake. Fainthearted bonds cannot last.

> *For if ye will not abide in my covenant ye are not worthy of me (D&C 98:15).*

To break the covenant is to stop cleaving to God, to break the embrace. He is always calling us in his direction. If we do wander away, he beseeches us to find our way back to the parental arms we left. "His hand is stretched out still" (Isaiah 9:17; 10:4; 1 Nephi 19:13–16). But if it is to be a real embrace, it must be mutual.

When such a perfectly trustworthy being gives his word, we notice. Our interest is awakened by knowing that he keeps promises and that he promises so much. His honesty is "an anchor of the soul, both sure and stedfast" (Hebrews 6:19; 6:17–18). He inspires trust. No wonder Nephi referred to the "many covenants of the Lord" as the "parts which are plain and most precious" of the ancient scriptures. And no wonder Satan schemed to have those very parts taken away in order to "blind the eyes and harden the hearts of the children of men" (1 Nephi 13:26–27). If we lose sight of God's personal vows to us, the gospel seems to lose size and beauty. So the prophets constantly beg us to be "mindful always of his covenant" (1 Chronicles 16:15; Exodus 24:7–8; Deuteronomy 4:23; 2 Kings 17:38; 23:2–3; 2 Chronicles 34:30). All sorts of reminders, forever pointing at the covenant, are built into gospel culture: ordinances, special days, the written word, meetings, buildings, and even clothing (Genesis 3:21; Deuteronomy 31:25–26; Joshua 3:3, 17; 1 Kings 6:19; 8:21; Moses 5:6–7; 6:63).

On the title page of the Book of Mormon, the Lord gives us an assignment. He says that his latter-day people should know "what great things the Lord hath done for their fathers; and that they may know the covenants of the Lord" (see also 2 Nephi 9:1). So what great things has he done for our ancient kindred?

Noah's family had the covenant we now have, and by means of it they were held in the Lord's hand. Consider the large clan of Jacob, surviving a famine and creating a legacy of faith against all odds. Think of Joseph being delivered from an Egyptian prison. Think of Lehi and Sariah coping with deserts and seas. The stories reach back and stretch on. They are stories of both deliverance and inheritance. We can read what God did for those of old, and we can believe that he will do the same for us (Isaiah 51:1–2; Helaman 3:30; D&C 132:37).

Few things are more worthy of our attention than to "know of the covenants of the Lord," which is a prime purpose of the Book of Mormon. And few goals are more worthy of our families than having the covenant written "in their inward parts, and . . . in their hearts" (Jeremiah 31:33). In this language of love, we invite him in.

Notes

1. *The Measure of Our Hearts* (Salt Lake City: Deseret Book, 1991), 72.
2. In Neal A. Maxwell, *If Thou Endure It Well* (Salt Lake City: Bookcraft, 1996), 121.

Chapter 8

GLIMPSES

Like a relentless heartbeat deep within the human spirit, our premortal fascination with family—our loyalty to the Father's timeless plan—will never go away. These three glimpses illustrate that point.

A FATHER'S PROPOSAL

David was a well-respected corporate executive when he retired. Now he and his wife could pursue some long-awaited dreams. But just as those dreams were about to come true, their son Brian was diagnosed with a crippling and possibly terminal illness.

While attending school, Brian had been working a night job doing unskilled labor. Though his income was modest, his work schedule accommodated his schooling, and the job provided medical benefits for his little family.

Brian's condition, along with the medical treatments he was receiving, eventually made it impossible for him to work, which in turn threatened his income and medical coverage.

After counseling about Brian's predicament, his parents struck upon a plan: David would come out of retirement and offer to work in Brian's place. This unusual arrangement received approval from Brian's employer and from the company providing medical insurance. A day or two later, David, the retired executive, found himself doing manual labor eight hours a night for several months during his son's struggle to recover.

David viewed his return to work as a blessing. With some emotion and a shining smile, he spoke of the privilege of doing for his son what his son could not do for himself.

No doubt David and Brian were acquainted with each other in the premortal life but only as brothers. Now they were father and son, faced with the kind of sobering twist that so often permeates mortal life. David, the former brother, was now a father. As a sibling, he might have offered sympathy to Brian's family. But as a participant in our Father's great plan, he dropped everything and offered himself.

BART'S HIDDEN INSTINCT

Bart was a young, single fellow when he joined the Church. He was a pleasant young man, but his former immersion in the world made certain gospel doctrines about marriage and family hard for him to accept at first. Even the presence of little children in sacrament meeting tried his faith. How would he ever survive a lifetime of meetings punctuated by crying babies, not to mention noisy little ones of his own someday?

But as the months passed, living the commandments prompted a radical change in Bart. He took a big step when he asked the bishop if there was any way he could teach in the Primary. With that experience, the floodgates of family feeling finally opened. It wasn't long before he was asking himself about a particular girl he was dating, "Will she be a good mother, and will she want a large family as I do?"

FAMILY, OF COURSE

Betty was seventy-one and her husband, Don, was seventy-three when they realized that their one-year-old granddaughter was going to need a new home—perhaps permanently. They knew there were agencies and programs that might take over, but none of this made sense to them. The only thing that made sense was to have that little girl join them in their little mobile home.

A whole lot of comfort was subtracted from their golden years in that one decision. It took them back forty years or so to again have a toddler around the home and yard, to chase that youngster down the aisles of the grocery store and meetinghouse, to have toys on the floor, diapers to change, Primary lessons to review, little meals to prepare, immunizations to get, prayers to teach, books to read, social skills to impart, attention and affection to give—both day and night. In the twilight years, they started over.

Why do all this for one who was but another sibling in the vast community of mankind? At the question, Betty glanced at her husband, smiled, looked back, and said, "Well, family, of course." Don nodded, "Yep. I don't guess it was a hard decision. Betty's right. Family."

Gathered with Our Fathers

The word of God . . . shall . . . land their souls, yea, their immortal souls, at the right hand of God in the kingdom of heaven, to sit down with Abraham, and Isaac, and with Jacob, and with all our holy fathers, to go no more out (Helaman 3:29–30).

The earthly history of the covenant is a sacred story. We who enter the covenant are aligned with the greatest souls of sacred history. We cast our lot with the noble and great ones (D&C 138:55; Abraham 3:22).

In Part Two we look to these giants and the promises they received. Whether or not we are their descendants, we and our families may become their heirs. No matter where or when we live, no matter how far from their faith we were once scattered, we can be gathered with them where they are now.

Chapter 9

"The Offering"

The covenant admits us to a timeless association of noble people and bestows an enormous legacy of great moments. The illustration that begins Part Two, a drawing titled "The Offering," commemorates those frequent times when our first parents knelt and remembered the covenant that was their hope. (In some ways, the illustration integrates the seven parts of this book.)

The heavy rocks of the altar remind us of eternity. It is from that stable source that we inherit the patterns of marriage and family. The rock also represents the Savior, upon whom every home must be built in order to stand through the rains and floods of the world. (Part One is titled "Built on Eternity.")

The husband and wife are our earthly roots. They are the ultimate earthly couple, representing the very best in all other couples since their day. The companionship we once saw in Heavenly Parents was translated into daily life by Adam and Eve. From them descended a rich history of sacred promises and devoted families. That history is our inheritance, our gathering point, our legacy, our family tradition. (Part Two is "Gathered with Our Fathers.")

The fire on the altar reminds us of a sweet warmth that draws us together into families, spouse to spouse, parent to child, generation to generation.

It is not just a physical or psychological force. The attraction is spiritual and sacred. (Part Three is called "Welded by Fire.")

We might wonder what Adam and Eve prayed about most. Every faithful parent knows the answer: their children. Where are the children in this painting? First, they are in the hearts of the couple, giving them every reason to reach upward ever so earnestly (suggested by Adam's posture) and bow ever so humbly (portrayed by Eve's posture). Second, the children (for example, you and I standing near this scene) are looking on, contemplating the prayer of their parents and wondering about entering into the covenant themselves. (Part Four of this book is titled "Joined by Children.")

The altar is a place of offering, a place of giving and forgiving. Adam and Eve offer themselves—their hearts and everything they have—to the Lord. In addition, the sacrifice on the altar is a similitude of the Lord's offering to them—his heart and everything he has. All this giving is to the family what light is to a house. It is grace and truth—the tenderness and patience, insight and reassurance, giving and forgiving—that makes home into heaven. (Part Five is called "Filled with Light.")

The scene also depicts order and solitude. Husband and wife kneel, facing each other across an altar that has been carefully assembled. The sacrifice is offered according to specific divine commands. They are praying in privacy, undisturbed. They will arise from prayer to live and work with wisdom and care, conducting life as much as possible as God would if he were in their place. All this stability is just one more way to invite the Lord to join them at home with his extra security and power. (Part Six is "Surrounded by Home.")

The altar is a place not only of sacrifice but also of promises. If we honor our promises, we know the Lord will keep his. He pledges to save us as well as our families. A couple at an altar reminds us of the highest gospel ordinances—those that carry the seal of heaven and the promise of family salvation. (Part Seven, the concluding section, is titled "Sealed to Heaven.")

Chapter 10

The Blessings of the Fathers

The covenant becomes a fullness when it is crowned with marriage vows.

Celestial marriage is the crowning ordinance of the gospel, the crowning ordinance of the house of the Lord (Bruce R. McConkie).[1]

This crowning ordinance stirs our sleeping identity, opens our veil, and unlocks our creation. Celestial marriage is not a finish line; rather, it is the beginning of a new eternity. It bestows the gift of children. It offers "the blessings of the fathers" (Abraham 1:2).

We . . . seek the blessings of the fathers as did Abraham by going to our Father's house. They are received in no other place on this earth (Ezra Taft Benson).[2]

The blessings of the fathers are the blessings of the Father himself. The Father's covenant admits earthly couples into a community of mortals and immortals who are being groomed for the ministry and destiny of their Heavenly Parents (D&C 107:19). They are in the bosom of Abraham and Sarah, Isaac and Rebekah, Jacob and Rachel, Adam and Eve, and a host of other exalted couples—full of possibilities, evolving to be just like their parents (Luke 16:22; D&C 2:3; 132:37).

Angels come down, combine together to gather their children, and gather

> *them. We cannot be made perfect without them, nor they without us (Joseph Smith).*[3]

The covenant is the Father's plan translated into a way of life (D&C 131:1–3). It brought our Eternal Parents together and unites them still. It holds everything else together as well. It is the heart of things. The covenant made our premortal heaven a home. It makes a mortal home into a heaven (Moses 1:39; D&C 132:6, 21).

So it stands to reason that "the work of the Father" is "preparing the way for the fulfilling of his covenants" (1 Nephi 14:17; 2 Nephi 29:14; 3 Nephi 21:4, 7, 26–29; Ether 4:14, 17). A lesser being would not and could not help us keep the covenants. A lesser being could not even keep them himself, for that matter. But the Father pays attention to myriad situations in myriad families. His work would be a colossal one even if there had been no apostasy, even if not one family had been scrambled since the days of Adam and Eve.

Yet the Father is never in the slightest part discouraged. He is buoyant. In fact, late in history, at the very point when time seems to have run out, his work is set to accelerate. Just when will momentum shift in favor of the blessings of the fathers? We have all sorts of clues. When the Nephite testimony comes to light, when Israel learns the gospel again, when a free nation takes shape against all odds, when the true Church is back on the job, when the improbable gathering starts, when prophets are called, when the abominations of Satan are countered by the power of God, . . .

> *When these things come to pass . . . it shall be a sign unto them, that they may know that the work of the Father hath already commenced unto*

the fulfilling of the covenant which he hath made unto the people who are of the house of Israel (3 Nephi 21:7; 20:12; 21:26; Ether 4:17).

The mammoth project has "already commenced," right on schedule. The ageless covenant is restored, keys are turning, and doors are opening for the first time in two thousand years. Many of us are entering, accepting the offerings of the Father and the Son, and making our own offerings. The most ambitious reclamation project we know of anywhere in the universe is underway.

For the eternal purposes of the Lord shall roll on, until all his promises shall be fulfilled (Mormon 8:22; 8:26).

The universe is a support system behind the blessings of the fathers, giving a sacred mission to material things (1 Nephi 22:3, 6; D&C 29:34; 49:16–17; 59:16–20; Abraham 3:24–26). The earth itself is a tabernacle, a home, for families. Covenant peoples and covenant families are on special terms with earth and history. Their lands are covenant lands, where they prosper according to their faithfulness rather than by strength and luck (Genesis 13:15; Exodus 6:8; Matthew 5:5; 1 Nephi 4:14; 2 Nephi 1:5, 20; 2 Nephi 4:4).

More astounding than the universe itself, as a support to the plan of the Father, is the atonement of the Son.

Then are ye sanctified in Christ by the grace of God, through the shedding of the blood of Christ, which is in the covenant of the Father unto the remission of your sins, that ye become holy, without spot (Moroni 10:33).

Along with everything else blood does in the physical body, it cleanses thoroughly. Cleansing is just what we need. Objects to be welded must first be cleaned. The blood of Christ takes away the soil and replaces it with a seal. It makes the covenant an instrument of mercy (Matthew 26:28; JST, Hebrews 9:20; Mosiah 5:5; 3 Nephi 20:26). His holy blood circulates to the cold extremities so that repentant persons and faint couples and wobbly families really can keep the covenant. Its influence warms people and gives them a surprising ability to live as they once could not even imagine living. Its miracle transforms feelings of alienation into a sense of belonging—belonging to the heavenly family again, belonging to the Savior who had once been a Brother but had become a stranger. Once we belong to Christ, he can give us to each other.

> *I would that ye should be steadfast and immovable, . . . that Christ . . . may seal you his, that you may be brought to heaven (Mosiah 5:15).*

Notes

1. In Conference Reports of The Church of Jesus Christ of Latter-day Saints (Salt Lake City: The Church of Jesus Christ of Latter-day Saints, April 1970), 27.
2. "What I Hope You Will Teach Your Children about the Temple," *Ensign,* August 1985, 9–10.
3. *Teachings of the Prophet Joseph Smith,* sel. Joseph Fielding Smith (Salt Lake City: Deseret Book, 1976), 159.

Chapter 11

KEY MOMENTS IN HISTORY

Earth's history is occasionally graced with couples whose lives are symbolic. In knowing about them, we understand something about heavenly things and even about our Heavenly Parents. With these couples we hope to someday be coheirs and companions (2 Nephi 3:12).

> *He shall plant in the hearts of the children the promises made to the fathers, and the hearts of the children shall turn to their fathers (D&C 2:2; 138:47).*

"The promises made to the fathers" inspire optimism within us and affection for the wonderful people who received them (D&C 128:18; 3 Nephi 5:25). We know the names of only a few of the faithful, but by learning about these few, we understand the hearts of all (Leviticus 26:42; Exodus 3:6; Luke 13:28; Alma 5:24; D&C 98:32).

Even the creation account is intertwined with ancestral names: Adam and Eve. The first people were none other than a *couple,* the ultimate symbol of our Father's plan. The first earthly meeting between two members of our race was the introduction of Eve to Adam. There were no primitive mumblings, no inept, growling attempts at language. Adam spoke, saying:

> *Therefore shall a man leave his father and his mother, and shall cleave unto his wife: and they shall be one flesh (Genesis 2:24; Moses 3:24).*

Adam's majestic statement was drawn from the everlasting covenant itself.

> *These words were . . . very likely the words spoken by Adam reciting the vows of the first marriage upon this earth. . . . Here was a marriage performed by the Lord between two immortal beings. . . . They were to be one throughout the eternal ages (Harold B. Lee).*[1]

The story of mankind rightly began with a romance. And this is how the covenant begins again in every generation. Every marriage of hope is another key moment in history (JST, Genesis 9:25; Moses 3:7; Abraham 1:3).

About two thousand years after Adam and Eve left the Garden of Eden, another important marriage story unfolded. Abram and Sarai were from unbelieving homes in a sordid place called Ur. These young people fortunately had records from their faithful ancestors. The words beckoned Abram and Sarai to come with "the fathers" unto the Son and to receive all that the Father hath.

They learned that the core of eternal life is marriage and parenthood, the privilege of God himself. They saw that service is not just a duty for those who seek rewards. It *is* the reward. They realized that a part of eternal life is offering it to others.

The young couple learned not to be surprised by trials. But through every trial they lived in harmony with the sacred records.

By tiny increments, the "doctrine of the priesthood" distilled (D&C 121:45). Finally, at the hands of Melchizedek, they received the full covenant. On that day of unspeakable satisfaction, while yet in the flesh, they commenced a heavenly career.

In an unpromising world, Abram and Sarai had sought for the covenant. They had pled for it, lived for it, embraced it, and stayed true. In the end, as a kind of president and matron of holy things, they could administer it to others (Abraham 1:2). The covenant was to be headquartered in their family and yet offered to all families. The Abrahamic line was to be a spiritual support system for mankind (1 Chronicles 16:15–17). Over the centuries, many were brought "into the bond of the covenant" by these administrators (Ezekiel 20:37). The effort of one couple is still growing into a gift for billions.

As Nephi hungered to know what his father knew, as the soul of Enos hungered to harvest the seed planted in him by the words of his father, so we may all inherit the quest of Abram and Sarai (1 Nephi 10:17; Enos 1:1). One hunger, the desire to be like our family heroes, leads to another hunger, the desire to know the God they found (Abraham 2:12). And, of course, once we have made our own discovery of him, we can pass that quest along to our children. It is a legacy of sacred longings (Genesis 26:24; Deuteronomy 29:13; 1 Nephi 6:4; 3 Nephi 12:6).

Abraham summarized the legacy in three drawings, which we now know as Facsimiles 1, 2, and 3 in the Book of Abraham. The first shows him on an altar, with the knife of a wicked man poised over his chest. Facsimile 1 corresponds with the spiritual jeopardy that hangs over all weak mortals. But the third facsimile shows Abraham on a throne, reminding us of the exaltation that awaits us after our altars.

Facsimile 2, which alludes to the ordinances of the gospel, gets us from the altar of Facsimile 1 to the throne of Facsimile 3. Abraham commends that path to us. He commends it to us as "the fathers" before him commended it to him (Genesis 17:4; Isaiah 51:1–2; 2 Nephi 8:1–2). You and I will commend it to others yet unborn. Perhaps they will one day look upon us as Abraham looked upon "the fathers."

> *If ye were Abraham's children, ye would do the works of Abraham (John 8:39).*

The grandsons and granddaughters of that once-obscure and childless couple are now like fathers and mothers to mankind. They mingle and serve among the nations. They take an interest and make a difference. They assist and lead (JST, Genesis 17:9–14; Helaman 3:30). And this is only a beginning.

> *If thy children will keep my covenant and my testimony that I shall teach them, their children shall also sit upon thy throne for evermore (Psalm 132:12).*

After their good influence has cascaded through the generations of this world, it will continue through endless generations hereafter. Members of the covenant-keeping line will at last come to their eternal thrones. This will make Abraham the father of countless fathers and Sarah the mother of countless mothers (Abraham 3:14). And it will make us as they are.

Note

1. *Decisions for Successful Living* (Salt Lake City: Deseret Book, 1973), 125.

Chapter 12

A Family That Serves Families

The Lord had a delight in thy fathers to love them, and he chose their seed after them, even you above all people (Deuteronomy 10:15).

The children of covenant parents are the "holy seed" (Ezra 9:2; Isaiah 6:13; 2 Nephi 16:13). Through them, the Father's way of life can be transferred to all parents and all children. This may seem like elitism, but in the long run it is just the opposite. The purpose of a holy lineage is not to exclude people outside the family but rather to labor at bringing everyone in. "Every living creature . . . for perpetual generations," every last soul in the universe, is on the calendar (Genesis 9:12, 17; 1 Nephi 13:23). We should remember that they who are not of Abraham are nevertheless of Someone holier. They will not fall through his fingers (Revelation 7:9, 14, 17).

Jesus once spoke in parable of this matter. A father-king set out a great feast. Not everyone was included in the first wave of invitations, but, as it turned out, this was only a matter of sequence. *All* the citizens would eventually be bidden, and the food would be as choice for the last guests as for anyone else (Matthew 22:1–10). It befits the first guests to be good and grateful ones and to help gather those whose turn comes next.

I make this covenant . . . with him that standeth here with us this day before the Lord our God, and also with him that is not here with us this day (Deuteronomy 29:14–15).

The covenant descends from one generation to the next by faithfulness (Genesis 17:9; 26:2–5; 48:3–4; Acts 3:25; D&C 132:37). The covenant passed from Abraham to Isaac only because Isaac kept it with all his heart, as did Isaac's son Jacob a generation later. To inherit the covenant is to inherit only an opportunity. Those of the holy seed cannot afford to bask in the stories of their mothers and fathers. The heritage survives only if there is new heroism.

We have made covenants. We made them before we accepted our position here on earth (Spencer W. Kimball).[1]

Birth into Israel comes not by things done in the flesh. The holy seed, at some time past, made a choice. To be born in a covenant home is a call, issued according to former tests. Once that station is granted, another test begins (Exodus 19:4–6; Acts 17:24–26; Romans 9:11; 2 Timothy 1:9; Alma 13:3; Abraham 3:23).

Israel is an eternal people. Members of that chosen race first gained their inheritance with the faithful in the pre-mortal life. Israel was a distinct people in the pre-existence. Many of the valiant and noble spirits in that first estate were chosen . . . to be natural heirs of all of the blessings of the gospel (Bruce R. McConkie).[2]

Israel is a kinship dating back through eons. Lineage does not create this royal people. Genetic links are the result, not the cause (Alma 13:3–4, 10).

God saw these souls that they were good, . . . and he said: These I will make my rulers (Abraham 3:23).

Israel is the most wonderful community in the universe. It draws membership from all times and peoples. A cross section of the righteous from every generation past will be gathered before Christ at his coming (D&C 133:54–55). Joseph F. Smith saw this same historic diversity gathered around "Father Adam" and "Mother Eve" in a "vast congregation" in the spirit world (D&C 138:38–39, 40–55). Apostles from one era and patriarchs from another are friends in exactly the same work, kin of the same covenant family, heirs of the same kind of salvation, ministering to relatives they all have in common (D&C 138:36–37).

In the writings of Abraham, we find the golden thread of the covenant, the purpose guiding the worldwide labors of his offspring: the children of Abraham *bless families* (their own as well as those of the stranger).

> *And in thy seed after thee . . . shall all the families of the earth be blessed (Abraham 2:11; Acts 3:25).*

The whole family of Israel—and each family in Israel—is to be a "peculiar treasure," a redemptive tool in the hands of Christ (Exodus 19:5). They are his light to the world. They are subordinate saviors, the children of the prophets, a preservative among earthly families who might otherwise spoil (Obadiah 1:17, 21; Romans 9:4; 3 Nephi 12:13–14; 20:25; D&C 86:11).

> *Thou art my servant, O Israel, in whom I will be glorified (1 Nephi 21:3).*

God gives to mankind his servant, the Messiah, and his great family of servants, Israel (1 Nephi 15:18; 21:1–2, 8–9). The word *family* is considered a derivation from a Celtic root, *famul,* meaning servants.[3]

The Book of Mormon has two prevailing messages: the divinity of Israel's Messiah, the Anointed One, and the destiny of the Messiah's Israel, the family of promise (Book of Mormon title page). The prophet Mormon concluded his writings with these two themes (Mormon 7). They echo through all the revelations like complementary notes in a musical chord.

Like Abraham and Sarah, we have books of great "worth . . . unto the making known of the covenants" (1 Nephi 22:9). It is our privilege to pore over our scriptures as those two hungry souls anciently feasted upon the sacred records bequeathed to them. In our holy books, we discover and rediscover the same robust, astounding themes that have been there all along: the family and the living Christ.

Notes

1. "Elijah Fulfilled Vital Mission in Eternal Plan," *Church News*, 18 December 1993, 14.
2. *Doctrinal New Testament Commentary*, 3 vols. (Salt Lake City: Bookcraft, 1965–73), 2:284.
3. *Noah Webster's First Edition of an American Dictionary of the English Language* (1828; republished in facsimile, San Francisco: Foundation for American Christian Education, 1967), s.v. "family."

Chapter 13

GATHERING: TURNING TO THE LORD

If thou turn to the Lord thy God, . . . he will not forsake thee . . . nor forget the covenant of thy fathers (Deuteronomy 4:30–31).

Turning to the Lord is not grim duty or cold routine, for it is the heart that does the turning. The covenant has always been a function of the heart (Jeremiah 31:33; Luke 1:16–17; 1 Nephi 19:14–15). Else how could we, every seventh day, promise to "always remember him" (D&C 20:77, 79)? Constant focus on the Savior has little to do with powers of concentration and everything to do with caring—a quality of the heart rather than a quantity of the mind. He responds in kind. To always have his Spirit is to have his attention, greeting, and companionship. He gives eminently more to the mutual remembering than we do. This is heart.

Once seeing the role of the heart, we may be surprised that the covenant also has a real estate department. But there have always been lands of promise, where people could join their hearts *together* in keeping promises.

We turn to the Lord best when we are alongside others who want to do the same. We override one culture by joining another. Without the principle of gathering, we would be trying to prepare for eternal worlds in isolation. The lonely approach is backward, wasteful, and self-centered.

If we lived in a day when God asked his people to migrate to a distant place, the journey would sanctify us if we let it. But if we are not crossing mountains or oceans, that is all right too. The "gathering" that must go forward in a branch or ward or within the four walls of a covenant home offers all the best features of a long trek. We will still face the unfamiliar, cross spiritual distances and human borders, and undertake superhuman tasks. We will still need patience and planning, worthiness and work, miracles and might. Either kind of gathering process serves as a perfect "lab" to go along with the ordinances. Together, the gathering and the ordinances lead to a fulness.

> *There are certain ordinances and principles that . . . must be done in a place or house built for that purpose. . . . It is for the same purpose that God gathers together His people in the last days (Joseph Smith).*[1]

We gather to *enter* the covenant, primarily in chapels and temples. We gather to *keep* the covenant, primarily in homes. Places of promise making and promise keeping are holy places (3 Nephi 21:4; 29:1).

Gathering refines us because it elevates us above the purely temporal life. To prosper in the land can be lethal unless the heart turns to Christ. This is evident in the Book of Mormon (2 Nephi 5:21; Jacob 2:17–19; Helaman 12:1–2). The earning of riches seems to get along fine with the covenant, but the yearning for riches is another matter. Materialism ruins everything (1 Timothy 6:10; D&C 6:7).

Consider the worthy example of our ancestor Abraham. When the time came to gather in a new place, Abraham shared the vast land of inheritance by offering first choice to his nephew Lot (Genesis 13:8–17).

Lot chose the plot that flowed with milk, honey, and money. What remained for Abraham and Sarah appeared neither pretty nor profitable. But what of that? Here one could live the gospel with all one's heart. It was arid, but seen through covenant eyes it was a paradise.

We might ask why Lot would want to go into a culture so oppressively corrupt as the cities of the plain—Sodom and Gomorrah. What was so attractive? Material things, no doubt. Lot's wife also likely figured into the decision to choose the well-watered but worldly plain. This is the lady who would someday look back, longing for her estate full of things in the city of Sodom. She and Lot would have been far better-off going with Abraham, wherever he went. But their real love was for material things. What they finally got was just what materialism always delivers in the end: a lot of nothing (Genesis 19:17, 24–28).

Covenant people should have a covenant place. To find such a place shapes history. But the greater achievement is to reserve sacred ground in the heart and to make Christ our landmark at home (Proverbs 22:28). Like Israel gathered around the great rock called Sinai, a covenant family is completely gathered only when clustered around their Redeemer.

This is also true in the world of spirits, where Christ is the gathering point (D&C 138:14–16). Dying is sometimes depicted as being gathered unto one's people. This is what the covenant holds for the faithful (Genesis 25:8; 35:27–29; 49:29, 33). The ultimate gathering is a family turned to Christ, whether living in this world or in the next.

> *These men are in heaven, but their children are on the earth. Their bowels yearn over us. . . . [They] combine together to gather their children. . . . We cannot be made perfect without them, nor they without us; when these things are done, the Son of Man will descend (Joseph Smith).*[2]

Notes

1. *Teachings of the Prophet Joseph Smith,* sel. Joseph Fielding Smith (Salt Lake City: Deseret Book, 1976), 308.
2. Ibid., 159.

Chapter 14

SCATTERING: DESOLATE DWELLINGS

Christ can do all his will—redeeming and saving beyond our fondest dreams—in a marriage or family that is "one." He looks for a certain kind of unity, the kind that agrees with him and gathers around him (D&C 6:32; 42:3). Rejecting his offering or his law or his servants or his church or his assignments are all ways of rejecting him (D&C 39:5). With covenant people he pleads, "How often would I have gathered you" (D&C 43:24; Matthew 23:37–39; 3 Nephi 10:4–7).

If ye are not one ye are not mine (D&C 38:27).

The only alternative to being gathered is to be scattered—broken up, set adrift. All it takes to be scattered is to turn away, to ignore the Master (Deuteronomy 28:58, 64; 1 Nephi 19:7; 11:35–36; 22:3–6).

When covenant people are scattered, their privileges are postponed, and they are disconnected from each other. It is no accident. Scattered people are "led away" on purpose, according to a far-reaching plan. Their loss is a means, not an end; a start, not a finish (1 Nephi 22:12). Scattering anticipates gathering. It is a complex tool in the hands of God "in bringing about his covenants" (1 Nephi 22:11). When the covenant-bearing lineage is transplanted, it may perhaps be humbled.

Of course, the Lord prefers handier and happier devices. He would rather assign the movements of his people with their families whole and their blessings intact. Scattering is a last resort (Deuteronomy 29:24–28; 1 Nephi 22:5).

What is true of a covenant people is true of a covenant family: they can be kept together only if their hearts are facing in the one right direction (D&C 54:4–5). The currents that split people apart do not wait until everyone is callous or complacent. A community can be severed by the few. This is especially true when prophets are taken lightly, for the Lord's ambassadors are sent to whole groups (Matthew 10:40; John 13:20; D&C 1:14; 88:36–37, 44). Whenever a branch of Israel neglects those messengers, it shrivels like the pinched-off limb of a plant (Matthew 23:37; John 15:1–7). Ironically, they are eventually judged by the apostles who once seemed so unimportant to them (1 Nephi 12:8–10, 18).

We are in or we are out. The plan of mercy covers us only if we keep our word (Mosiah 1:13). In the covenant, we ride upon superhuman forces that move us either upward or downward. We succeed, or else the enemy does. If Israel keeps its promises, it lives up to the meaning of its name: "prevailing with God."

> *I will give peace in the land. . . . And five of you shall chase an hundred, and an hundred of you shall put ten thousand to flight. . . . I will have respect unto you . . . and establish my covenant with you. . . . And I will set my tabernacle among you. . . . I will walk among you, and will be your God, and ye shall be my people (Leviticus 26:6, 8–9, 11–12).*[1]

Were these terms for people of olden times only? Of course not. Embedded squarely in the higher law of the latter days, the same prevail-or-fail covenant applies:

By hearkening to observe all the words which I . . . shall speak unto them, they shall never cease to prevail. . . . But inasmuch as they keep not my commandments, . . . the kingdoms of the world shall prevail against them (D&C 103:7–8).

The choice is between unity and dissolution. There is no level playing field as one might demand outside the covenant. The odds are high, either against us or for us. And when the Lord must remind forgetful people of who they are, sometimes he uses their family ties to do so (D&C 93:50).

How oft will I gather you . . . if ye will repent and return unto me. . . . But if not, O house of Israel, the places of your dwellings shall become desolate (3 Nephi 10:6–7; Jeremiah 29:10–14; Matthew 23:37–38).

Despite every sort of man-made protection, nothing is secure unless we keep the covenant. A whole people is liable to be scattered if they are not girded about in the Lord's own way. Without the holy shield, a specific family is scattered according to the same law. It may move slowly, but the scattering is sure. A house left desolate—unfriendly, bleak, alone—is a loss to overshadow all other losses.

If we go off on our own, disengaged from the covenant, we match the tender family circle against a steely, justice-driven universe. We might as well go naked into outer space. To take the covenant lightly is to go mercy-less, temple-less, and promise-less into eternity.

Note

1. This chapter of Leviticus also describes the unhappy results of dishonoring the covenant (verses 24–39); see also Deuteronomy 28.

Chapter 15

RESTORING THE ETERNAL

The two greatest realities we know anything about are divine offerings—the Father's plan and the Son's atonement. The covenant is our way of accepting those offerings. When covenant people forget, they are scattered. It is a hard lesson.

Only God can know when such a lesson is necessary. The Lord knew to scatter his people of the northern kingdom of Israel in 720 B.C., the southern kingdom of Judah in 588 B.C., the inhabitants of Jerusalem in 70 A.D., and those gathered at Cumorah in 385 A.D. In his wisdom, the lesson was taught again in Ohio and Missouri in the 1830s (D&C 101:6, 8).

I will make a new covenant with the house of Israel (Jeremiah 31:31).

Only God would know just when the hard lesson—whether imposed on a family or on a whole nation—has at last filled its purpose (3 Nephi 21:22–24). Under his eye, scattering eventually gives way to "times of refreshing" (Acts 3:19). The promise was serious: "How oft will I gather you" (3 Nephi 10:6; D&C 101:9).

So, after centuries of absence, the covenant has now been restored from its timeless place of origin, heaven itself. The old slumbering race of Abraham and Sarah begins to stir, "for they are not lost unto the Father, for he knoweth whither he hath taken them" (3 Nephi 17:4). We are being "gathered home," not only to a place but also to an old friendship "which should be fulfilled in the latter days" (1 Nephi 15:18; 2 Nephi 29:14).

The keys of the dispensation, which ye have received, have come down from the fathers (D&C 112:32).

People may now connect themselves to the Father in Heaven and the fathers on earth (D&C 27:9–11; 110:13–16; 128:17–18). And yet, wondrous as this is, the restoration is a curious sight to most of mankind, a turning of things right side up after centuries of being upside down (Isaiah 29:16). So gradually and unanimously has truth been replaced by error that its fresh introduction comes as a shock.

The great ship Israel unfurled her sails on a foreign shore, and she holds her course for another. We glimpse her plowing along, glowing unearthly in the mortal haze. She seems a bit strange on our dark little sea.

What I have said unto you must needs be, . . . that I may proceed to bring to pass my act, my strange act, and perform my work, my strange work (D&C 101:93–95; Habakkuk 1:5; D&C 18:44).

Of all the "strange" features of the covenant, we might marvel most at its endlessness. If the covenant were temporary, it would prove worthless in the end. But it has no end. Though it is *new* to each beginning recipient, each freshly created soul, it is also *everlasting*. This one blessing—permanence—is what makes all the other blessings utterly supernal, worth every cost.

If nothing else came out of all of the sorrow and travail and pain of the Restoration than the sealing power of the holy priesthood to bind together families forever, it would have been worth all that it has cost (Gordon B. Hinckley).[1]

What is worth every cost to the Church and the prophets is worth everything to you and me. Without Christ, the covenant could not last forever.

His work spreads the covenant. His light attracts the honest unto it. His voice introduces the covenant to minds and verifies it in hearts. His blessings make it satisfying here and joyous hereafter. Jesus is everything to the covenant.

> *The Lord, whom ye seek, shall suddenly come to his temple, even the messenger of the covenant, whom ye delight in (Malachi 3:1; 3 Nephi 24:1).*

We are summoned, called, beckoned, by Jesus, this "messenger of the covenant." His invitation will finally reach every willing home.

> *The voice of the Lord is unto all men, and there is . . . no . . . heart that shall not be penetrated. . . . I the Lord am willing to make these things known unto all flesh (D&C 1:2, 34).*

Little wonder modern prophets, soon after proclaiming to the world Christ's official message, titled "The Family—A Proclamation to the World," published their testimony of him, "The Living Christ." (The first was introduced in September 1995; the second is dated January 1, 2000). It is the ultimate gospel combination: the family (the Father's offering) and the family's Savior (the Son's offering).

We can go to Primary and hear the children sing out the deep wisdom in these images: a house, a bedrock, a storm, a promise that the house will not fall.[2] Jesus was emphatic about it. Homes must be built on his own rock—his atonement, his revelations, his priesthood, his ordinances, his covenant, his Church—in order to outlast the inevitable bad weather (3 Nephi 14:24–26; 11:38–41; 18:12–13; 2 Samuel 22:2–3; Psalm 18:2; 1 Nephi 13:36; D&C 11:24).

It is our privilege in the latter days to rely on the Rock. The wise man and woman, after entering the covenant, will build their house upon him.

Notes

1. *Teachings of Gordon B. Hinckley* (Salt Lake City: Deseret Book, 1997), 475–76.
2. "The Wise Man and the Foolish Man," *Children's Songbook* (Salt Lake City: The Church of Jesus Christ of Latter-day Saints, 1989), 281.

Chapter 16

GLIMPSES

These glimpses from the past—provided by the New Testament—represent countless incidents that testify of the family theme in human history. The guiding principles behind these samples are without beginning of years or end of days.

A GRANDFATHER'S ANNOUNCEMENT

One of the most fascinating moments in the history of the covenant was the announcement of Christ's birth. The messenger was Gabriel, who was none other than Noah.

> *Noah, who is Gabriel . . . stands next in authority to Adam in the Priesthood; he was called of God to this office, and was the father of all living in this day (Joseph Smith).*[1]

The news was given first to Zacharias, who was to be the father of John the Baptist. Zacharias was later inspired by the Holy Ghost to speak about the Messiah's coming in the flesh. Even inspired words cannot quite do justice to the importance of this birth, but in trying to measure this magnificent event, Zacharias said:

> *Blessed be the Lord God of Israel; for he hath visited and redeemed his people . . . to perform the mercy promised to our fathers, and to remember his holy covenant (Luke 1:68, 72).*

It is fitting that Gabriel would be the bearer of this news. Because he was the father of all living in his day, he is the father of everyone who lived after his day. So when he came to Zacharias and later to Mary and Joseph, Gabriel was bringing big news to his big family, his own descendants.

He once warned of worldwide destruction. He once stepped off the ark onto a newly cleansed earth and restarted the covenant for all future history (JST, Genesis 9:15, 18–25). Now, as the ultimate grandfather, he was announcing the Rescuer of worldwide kindreds, tongues, and peoples. He called the attention of his grandchildren to their One Hope. The Family Friend was coming, just as promised.

The Timeless Invitation

My son Joseph was kind enough to provide the beautiful image on the front of this book, which he has named *Inviting Him In.* This illustration brings to mind the two followers of Jesus who were walking to Emmaus (Luke 24:13–35). The two, who some scholars believe were a married couple, were downcast about the confusing end to Jesus' life. But along the way they encountered a wondrous Teacher who expounded the scriptures and unfolded the meaning of the whole law of covenants, commandments, and faith.

When the two reached their destination, they might have let their Companion go on. But having felt a burning in their hearts as he talked to them "by the way," and sensing the value of his friendship and wisdom, they invited him in. His blessing, no doubt, came upon them during his short stay. And if, in fact, they were a married couple, his blessing came upon their family as well.

One thing we know for sure. Jesus did not leave them until they were reminded, by the breaking of the bread, of their covenant. Only then, when their eyes were opened, did they realize the identity of their Guest.

Figuratively speaking, any of us could be standing in a doorway in Emmaus, determined to invite him in—including a couple pleading for his divine help, a wife or husband asking for his companionship in a hopeful vigil for others in the home, or a prodigal son or daughter inviting him back into their lives.

We invite him in as we try to remove the barriers separating our household from his blessed and blessing presence.

Note

1. *Teachings of the Prophet Joseph Smith,* sel. Joseph Fielding Smith (Salt Lake City: Deseret Book, 1976), 157.

WELDED BY FIRE

Therefore shall a man leave his father and his mother, and shall cleave unto his wife (Genesis 2:24).

The fire that brings delight and oneness into family relationships is a sacred tool for oneness. It even inspires us to seek at-one-ment. The fire remains bright and holy as long as it stays where God intended it to be, on the altar of the covenant. It is a power of attraction that draws us into families and a power of affection that keeps us warm in a bitter and icy world (D&C 88:40). Without this family warmth, the gospel itself can seem cold for some of our loved ones. With the holy fire where it belongs, everything that is important stays together (Matthew 19:6).

Not everyone is currently free to enjoy the affections and roles explored in this chapter. Their family relationships may now be anything but affectionate. And yet, winter is temporary. Every warmth, joy, bond, and fulfillment discussed in these chapters—the fulness of the sacred fire—awaits all the faithful in eternity if not in time. The springtime is sure.

Chapter 17

A Flame from Heaven

We were created to be attracted to each other. Children are naturally attracted to the authority and strength of adults. Adults naturally devote themselves to little children. The aged enjoy sharing their wisdom, while the young and inexperienced enjoy listening. And, of course, shining near the center of all these native attractions is the appeal of gender itself.

This is all true if the covenant is intact. When the natural fires burn where they belong, mankind is friendly to the great plan of happiness. Soon after we depart the world of sibling premortality, the mortal world welcomes and adores us as it wraps and adorns us with new relationships. The Creator is priming us, inclining us toward our new loved ones. Then, with time, we are guided into a greater variety of ties and friendships as if by a glowing flame. Eventually we choose the covenant out of both faith and delight.

> *It is an offering made by fire, of a sweet savour unto the Lord (Leviticus 2:9).*

The solemn altar of the covenant would be bare without the fire of family affection. The warmth draws us together and holds us in place. Like all miracles, it is based on law—a law of attraction (D&C 88:40). But for the attraction to be pure, the heart must be pure. We acquire the great power of love by using all of our *other* powers unselfishly (Moroni 7:46–48). Purity supports the sacred privileges of the Father's plan.

See that ye bridle all your passions, that ye may be filled with love (Alma 38:12).

No wonder a direct connection exists between chastity and charity. The heavenly flame always warms but never harms. Charity looks with reverence upon a human soul. It lives and thinks in accordance with this reverence. In Jacob 2:17–28, a discourse on charity leads naturally to a discussion of chastity.

The unholy kind of fire is too one-sided to view others with reverence. It is too narrow to see whole persons. It cares only about fragments of people, viewing them simply as parts, objects, or tools. Unholy fire is unwhole. It burns for one person only—oneself (Jeremiah 19:5).

The Lord God caused a deep sleep to fall upon Adam, and . . . made . . . he a woman, and brought her unto the man (Genesis 2:21–22; Moses 3:21–22).

The typical young man is in a deep sleep. He hardly senses anything important until his future wife comes along. "Where did *she* come from?" he asks. He knew there were girls out there, but this particular one is not a mere prospect or prototype. She is the real thing. She seems to come out of nowhere because his eyes have opened in stages. (Even after marriage, he might doze off and on for years.) As he perceives this gift—his companion bestowed by God—it is as if he sees the rest of God's gifts to him for the first time. The Father's old plan seems new and larger than before.

In its very nature, sex is spiritual and inseparably connected with the creative work of God (Mark E. Petersen).[1]

Romantic attractions and powers are tied to the spirit itself. As

President McKay said, "When we touch the creative part of life, we enter into the realm of divinity."[2] And what is essentially spiritual is also powerful. Among the many types of family affection, the husband-wife force is the most sacred in its origins and its possible outcome. Besides creating lives, it brings to pass other kinds of affections, other kinds of links. It can be holy, comforting, and lasting. Or it can be unholy and deadly. So the standard, the distinct boundary set by God himself, is to never arouse those set-apart feelings in another person except within the marriage covenant and to never stimulate them in oneself at all.

> *Do not use the power prematurely, not with anyone (Boyd K. Packer).*[3]

> *Any sexual intimacy outside of the bonds of marriage—I mean any intentional contact with the sacred, private parts of another's body with or without clothing—is a sin and is forbidden by God. It is also a transgression to intentionally stimulate these emotions within your own body (Richard G. Scott).*[4]

In other words, that flame is kindled in men and women to warm, sustain, and beautify the covenant. When not on that mission, it does not sanctify. Instead, the fire is at best an incinerator, at worst a holocaust. (Lust, like dishonesty and anger, *dis*-invites Christ and blocks his entry.) And a deliberate arsonist—Satan, the archenemy of the Father's plan—urges the flames beyond their set bounds.

> *Within your body is the power to beget life. . . . The only legitimate expression of that power is within the covenant of marriage. The worthy use of it is the very key to your happiness (Boyd K. Packer).*[5]

Obviously, not all flames are evil. The attractions and affections of marriage and family relationships can be "sanctifying" (Joseph F. Smith).[6] As fire is used to temper imperfect metals, the private sharing of affection within marriage can add dignity and goodness to the souls of husband and wife. This sacred interaction calls for real consideration, esteem, and unselfishness.

> *Tenderness and respect—never selfishness—must be the guiding principles in the intimate relationship between husband and wife. Each partner must be considerate and sensitive to the other's needs and desires. Any domineering, indecent, or uncontrolled behavior in the intimate relationship between husband and wife is condemned by the Lord (Howard W. Hunter).*[7]

As heat is used ever so carefully to weld some substances, the holy flame between husband and wife can form a bond more durable than life itself.

Notes

1. In Conference Reports of The Church of Jesus Christ of Latter-day Saints (Salt Lake City: The Church of Jesus Christ of Latter-day Saints, April 1969), 63–64.
2. Ibid., 6.
3. *Let Not Your Heart Be Troubled* (Salt Lake City: Bookcraft, 1991), 50.
4. "Making the Right Choices," *Ensign,* November 1994, 38.
5. *Let Not Your Heart Be Troubled,* 50; see also D&C 49:16–17.
6. *Gospel Doctrine* (Salt Lake City: Deseret Book, 1986), 309.
7. *The Teachings of Howard W. Hunter* (Salt Lake City: Bookcraft, 1997), 134.

Chapter 18

Bigger than We Are

The scriptures constantly hint at the importance of marriage. But in Doctrine and Covenants section 132, the Lord does not just hint! His revelation to Joseph Smith leaves no question about the priority of marriage. The only question is whether we will align our *hearts* with his law (D&C 132:21). It is in the heart that we either go forward or stall in doing his will.

> *Prepare thy heart to receive and obey the instructions which I am about to give unto you (D&C 132:3).*

After this caution, the Lord unfolds his law of marriage. Once we are married, the covenant is designed to stretch our hearts to the size of his heart if we will let it. "Prepare thy heart" to bow before great principles in daily married life. God's kind of life—faith, good cheer, loyalty, unselfishness, and work at home—depends entirely on the right kind of heart.

The person whose marriage has not yet become a "celestial" one or the person who does not yet have a marriage at all can progress. We are all being encouraged to live the best we can right now in preparation for the fulness. He or she who follows those urgings eventually "cometh unto God" (D&C 84:47).

No circumstances, no matter how incompatible with our Father's ways, and no background or weakness, no matter how overpowering, can cancel this slow and subtle miracle. The person who keeps yearning for light and who keeps caring about that voice will eventually be groomed to fit into a heavenly home (2 Peter 1:4; D&C 76:42–43). The Lord indicated that some souls might take "all [their] days" to come unto him, and he made it clear that they are worth the effort. So we should not be too surprised if someone we know—including ourselves—is making very slow progress (D&C 18:15).

Marriage is ordained of God unto man (D&C 49:15).

Marriage is ideal for man. Marriage and humans go together. Members of our race—God's race, in fact—cannot be all that he intends until they enter into his "ordained" way of life.

Two lives become one life. The wife and husband, previously strangers in a thousand ways, carve out their little realm. Each new couple is as Adam and Eve, alone in their new world. They are to become more acquainted with each other than they are with anything or anyone else in the world. This means that they not only "leave father and mother" but also give friends and fascinations a lesser priority, or perhaps no priority at all (Matthew 19:5). Their freshly created household slowly builds confidence and power. Its destiny is to be a perfect and growing household forever.

They twain shall be one flesh, and all this that the earth might answer the end of its creation; and that it might be filled with the measure of man (D&C 49:16–17).

The earth itself was created to support the couple in their ordained career as parents. Unto the righteous, the earth yields the means of survival, security, and privacy (D&C 49:19; 59:17–19). The earth is a small subject compared to marriage.

The whole subject of the marriage relation is not in my reach, nor in any other man's reach on this earth. It is without beginning of days or end of years; it is a hard matter to reach (Brigham Young).[1]

Everything God has revealed about marriage suggests that it is bigger than we can now understand. Consider a few hints: it is rooted in eternity past; it is the gate to eternity future; it is designed to be as everlasting as the body and the spirit (D&C 132:19–20); it is a means for mortals to emulate eternal parents;[2] it does not just fit in with the covenant, but in certain ways it *is* the covenant; it is the very top of the very crown of the master plan; it is the ultimate arrangement for expressing fidelity and honor; it is the only means for creating souls and the perfect means for nurturing them; it sanctifies those who enter it and then remain true.

The lawful association of the sexes is ordained of God . . . for the development of the higher faculties and nobler traits of human nature, which the love-inspired companionship of man and woman alone can insure (Joseph F. Smith).[3]

In the wisdom of God, we are allowed to stumble into this order of things long before we can understand it. We are part of a drama to be fathomed long after we leave this world.

Marriage is the highest calling we will ever have. Few people in this world will notice if we succeed at it. The happiest outcomes are made public after the probation is over, after our chances have expired. For now, the surrounding culture will probably not punish us for a weak effort. Nor can we expect a worldly reward for giving our all to it. However, to fulfill the mission of marriage is like dropping a huge rock into heaven's living waters. Be ever so quiet and private if you want, but the ripples will grow as they cross the surface of eternity.

One of the few good reasons for leaving father and mother is to create the relationship we have prepared for not only during our mortal years but also during premortal ages past (Genesis 2:24; Ephesians 5:31). We may be tempted to hold back, thinking the solo life is simple and free of pain. But the corridors of history echo the unfailing lesson that we first heard from God himself: "It is not good that the man should be alone" (Genesis 2:18; Moses 3:18; Abraham 5:14).

Most of us will have a season of wintry isolation. But we should not allow ourselves to get too accustomed to it. Winter has its purposes, as does loneliness. But those purposes are passing; we must welcome the spring. What toughens and tempers us in small doses will shrink and deform if prolonged. In the long run, the life of one thrives best when blended thoroughly with another.

Before Eve came along, Adam was a prince in solitary confinement, forced to be the most comfy hermit in history. But it was better to go into the thorns with a queen's hand in his than to remain in vacuous wealth and ease without her. Neither he nor she could have joy and meaning without each other, not even if provided with a luxuriant garden, a smart parakeet, a noble dog, or even a good buddy with matching hobbies. A celestial companionship is not just two lives overlapping at many points. The sharing must be total and irreversible—two people living one complete life.

We were each created to complement another person who should *not* be just like us. We were made to form into couples.

The Father got each of us started, but our formation is still in process. To be finished, we must leave solitude behind forever. Getting married is to be our last and greatest solo achievement. It is fitting that we do this on our own initiative and without reservation. We pledge ourselves entirely to a mystery person. A slow and timid sweep of the sickle will not cut grass, nor can partial commitment to the covenant result in a complete soul or a polished marriage. The last phases of soul growth are mutual growth—learning the highest lessons together, doing the most important work together, and finally inheriting all things together.

Notes

1. In *Journal of Discourses,* 26 vols. (London: Latter-day Saints' Book Depot, 1854–86), 2:90.
2. *Encyclopedia of Mormonism: The History, Scripture, Doctrine, and Procedure of The Church of Jesus Christ of Latter-day Saints,* ed. Daniel H. Ludlow, et. al., 4 vols. (New York: Macmillan, 1992), s.v. "Family," 2:487.
3. In *Messages of the First Presidency of The Church of Jesus Christ of Latter-day Saints,* comp. James R. Clark, 6 vols. (Salt Lake City: Bookcraft, 1965–75), 5:64; *Improvement Era,* June 1917, 739; 4 Nephi 1:11.

Chapter 19

STAYING TOGETHER

After the decision to marry, there follows a lifetime of decisions about that marriage. Hour by hour, we decide the quality of our companionship, the level of loyalty, the extent of our love.

> *When you are married, be fiercely loyal one to another (Gordon B. Hinckley).*[1]

God appreciates the promise made, but he loves the promise kept. Loyalty is staying true, with enthusiasm. It is not just "sticking" together; it is being fully invested in another life, involved, alloyed, welded.

A flaw in some marriages is the "righteous" partner who is really only tolerant, who only endures. Polite neutrality softens no heart, invites no mighty change. A dull and lifeless faith wonders, "How long must I wait for this person to change?" An active faith asks, "What can I do to reach the heart of my companion?" A loving delight softens what mere endurance cannot. Tenderness opens doors that are locked to neutrality. Mercy may travel territory that is forbidden to justice.

Like other callings, marriage is a promised land, a field of possibilities awaiting our purchase (Matthew 13:44). At today's prices, what will this field cost? The cost of marriage has always been the same: everything. It is a good price. The treasure buried or veiled there is infinite. Why be afraid of a bargain like that?

We bear a striking resemblance to God when, instead of fretting about whether the decision was right, we roll up our sleeves and go to work to *make* things right. Such loyalty is divine. Even the finest raw materials are coarse and unremarkable to begin with. The master woodworker makes something beautiful out of the grain and shape, the knots and hardness.

The first couple stayed together despite a major upset—the Fall. They left the exquisite meadows and forests instead of leaving each other. They endured pain rather than parting.

A maiden of Mesopotamia, Rebekah of the city of Nahor, had such a choice. She could enter a covenant of marriage with righteous Isaac in far-off Canaan, or she could remain secure and well-off where she was. Her modest answer, "I will go," made sacred history. Faithful people by their steady integrity do that, molding history in the process (Genesis 24:55–58).

Some matches may not be promising at first, but the Lord considers us so pliant and progressive that he commands us to get married anyway. "The shedding of the blood of Christ, which is in the covenant of the Father," is designed to undo our fatal flaws and make us "holy, without spot" (Moroni 10:33). This enormous resource makes every covenant marriage a promising one after all.

God knows just how to get people together and to keep them together. He is the great combiner of souls. His miracles need time and patience, but with willing partners he can make a perfect union out of a faltering friendship.

> *What therefore God hath joined together, let not man put asunder" (Mark 10:9).*

When faith ebbs low, it is easy to put a trembling marriage asunder. Those who are preoccupied with the mortal weakness of a spouse seem to believe little about the changing power of Christ. Incessant criticism repudiates the faith that put them together in the first place. The result is the dark and false doctrine of a hopeless, Christ-less marriage.

Inasmuch as they break not my laws thou shalt bear their infirmities (D&C 42:52).

What is a Savior all about if not saving us from the infirmities of personality and habit? Does the Redeemer not really redeem? Jesus the Christ heals people and their relationships. His specialty is change. Why not invite him in and let him work?

It would be foolish, of course, to pretend that all marriages are going to be saved. Some are prisons. Some have been reduced to ashes. A marriage gone bad can be renewed and healed but only if it can exist at all. At the very least, it needs civility, fidelity, and charity.

Civility is simple human respect. It is true that one might choose to stick it out for a time amid incivility. But no person has a duty to submit to inhumane or indecent treatment. *Fidelity* is the desire to be together and to be loyal. When a partner has no intention to remain or to be faithful, the whole point of marriage has been abandoned. *Charity* of a minimal kind allows us to let go of harsh feelings. When past offences, real or imagined, cannot be set aside, when the principle of forgiveness is thrown out to make room for retaliation, the light of hope squeezes down to an ever-smaller pinhole.

What happens if the vital elements are missing? When the basic dignity of a person is at stake, it may be necessary to release that person from the gruesome grip. But it is not the role of anyone outside the marriage to make that decision. If the freedom to heal has been lost, if the ingredients of life are gone, if it is wise for a suffering spouse finally to leave, only that spouse can know that. That spouse, who must live with any unpleasant results that might follow even the most necessary divorce, is entitled to know the all-important factor in such a decision: timing. Should it be soon? How will timing affect the children? Should I give it more time? Some people can endure a famine longer than others.

Jesus said it was because of hard hearts that marriages in his day were dissolved. This cause lurks somewhere in most divorces of our day as well. Someone's heart grows resistant and inhospitable. Civility, fidelity, or charity may then shrivel in one partner or both. The Master pointed out, "But from the beginning it was not so" (Matthew 19:8). That is, the Father intended that neither partner should let this happen.

And if a marriage ends, what then? We go forward with faith. We go on inviting the Saving Friend to come in. Whether one partner or both have allowed hardness to afflict the heart, both should stay on the path of salvation even if they no longer walk it side by side. Christ can soften any heart, no matter how hard. He can heal any heart, no matter how broken. His gospel is all about trying again. Even if his blessing must come in another chapter, under another roof, in another chance at happiness with some other spouse, Jesus should still be invited in.

Thus when Jesus encountered the lady at the well in Samaria, knowing the story of her many marriages, he did not heap the past on her head. It was, in the end, *his* role to pay for her mistakes. He pled with her to recognize who he was, to invite him into her untidy world, and to begin partaking of his life-giving water (John 4:10, 13–14, 16–19, 25–26, 28–30, 39–42).

This child is set for the fall and rising again of many in Israel (Luke 2:34).

Well did the inspired Simeon speak when he saw the infant Messiah. By ignoring or forgetting him, people do fall. But that stern fact is joined by good tidings. Jesus is entirely "set," he is sincerely ready to *raise again* whoever might fall, whether they stumble by their own mistakes or trip by the fall of another.

> *He hath sent me to bind up the brokenhearted, to proclaim liberty to the captives, and the opening of the prison to them that are bound; . . . to comfort all that mourn; to appoint unto them that mourn in Zion, to give unto them beauty for ashes, the oil of joy for mourning. . . . They shall build the old wastes, they shall raise up the former desolations (Isaiah 61:1–4).*

Some are, for a season, homeless or allotted homes of woe or imprisoned in dark marriages. Along with his mission to all other brokenhearted persons, Christ is also sent to liberate these. He will liberate them in due time, and when he does he will replace their ashes with beauty.

The vast majority of struggling marriages *do* have the ingredients necessary for renewal. The Atoning One is supremely able to bring "at-one" those who were once at odds. We invite him in by working relentlessly at marital refinement instead of giving way to gloomy despair. The Lord is in the business of saving that which seems lost, and he delights in those who cooperate with all their hearts.

> *Be not weary in well-doing, for ye are laying the foundation of a great work. And out of small things proceedeth that which is great (D&C 64:33).*

Note

1. "Messages of Inspiration from President Hinckley," *Church News,* 2 September 1995, 2.

Chapter 20

MEET FOR EACH OTHER

Let us make an help meet for the man (Abraham 5:14).

Adam, known also as Michael, is first among the sons of earth, holding the priesthood keys "from generation to generation" (Joseph Smith).[1] He is clearly one of our Father's most sturdy and dependable sons. Yet he needed the kind of "help" that even the most faithful employee could never give. The companion sent to him was a full partner. She too was sterling and strong, one of the noble and great ones. In other words, she was "meet" for him.

The word *equal* would not say all that is carried by the word *meet*. To simply equate a man and woman suggests that, after some kind of analysis, they end up in a tie. But men and women differ too dramatically for comparison. They are as incomparable as seed and sun or wind and sail.

"Meet" means perfectly matched or suited. As Eve was meet for Adam, so he was meet for her. They were created to need each other, even in paradisiacal Eden and more especially in the demanding ages ahead.

The hand of God put this first couple together, establishing the pattern for countless other couples to follow. We each need someone to become meet for us just as we each need to become meet for someone else.

Our covenant career begins at baptism, when we embrace the offering of the Son. With this initial covenant we receive the companionship of the Holy Ghost. But we need to receive yet another offering and yet another companion. With marriage we receive another companion, a special kind of comforter, a person of faith who, like ourselves, is still under development—our spouse.

Companions have special roles by which they add to each other. In the unselfish blend of interests and strengths and gifts, the sum of two companions is not just two people. One covenant person can "chase a thousand" of the enemy when necessary, but *two* who are joined in the covenant are ten times as strong and can "put ten thousand to flight" (Deuteronomy 32:30; Matthew 18:19).

If unhappy spouses can do little else, they can at least remember that their part in a marriage is a calling before God, a calling to be magnified with faith and zeal. This will save and satisfy at least one person and will likely open the gates of happiness for two. Our roles make us meet for each other.

Without humility, neither man nor woman can quite succeed in their divine marital assignments. Both are to honor the priesthood—an act that usually demands more humility in the husband than in the wife (D&C 121:41–42). Though husband and wife use different means to manipulate, manipulation is always wrong. Each must restrain the human tendency to control another soul. Each must be tempered by obedience to that other companion, the Holy Ghost, who can teach so much about companionship (D&C 121:46).

To neglect one's role is to rebuff both companions—the marital one and the divine one. Being out of tune with the Spirit goes hand in hand with being out of touch with one's spouse. Each is part of the same unhappy cycle. The happy version of that cycle gets underway when we renew both kinds of fellowship (1 Corinthians 11:11). Change starts with communication—the kind that is humble, frank, respectful. Change also depends on a resolve, stronger than the cords of death, to do all of one's part—to live one's role in the relationship.

When societies suffer from apostasy, they get distorted views about marriage and gender. That confusion poisons everything it touches (JS–H 1:19). Both women and men become miserably confused about themselves and about each other (D&C 76:75). The purity of men, the sanctity of women, the holiness of home—these ideals dwindle away. Whole nations go to oblivion on this path (D&C 87:6).

As with scripture, so with society: plain and precious things are taken away from what originated in heaven (1 Nephi 13:26). Satan, who knows that the roles of men and women pertain to eternity, makes marriage his prime target (Genesis 3:15). He attacks not only marriage in general but also all the specifics, including the roles of husband and wife.

We can think of marriage as a mission shared equally by husband and wife. The core of the mission is *creation, edification,* and *decision.* For example, when the first husband and wife created the life of a new person, it was their privilege to edify that life. And constantly, they had things to *decide.* Even before they left the Garden, they had a big decision to make.

All couples must learn how to create, edify, and decide as if they were one person. And surrounding that core mission, each spouse has distinct roles to help make the mission a success. Their roles are destinies; they begin here and flourish hereafter.

> *By divine design, fathers are to preside over their families in love and righteousness and are responsible to provide the necessities of life and protection for their families. Mothers are primarily responsible for the*

nurture of their children (The First Presidency and Council of the Twelve Apostles).[1]

If a couple needs raw materials to fulfill their mission, the husband is to *provide* them. If dangers and opponents lurk at the doorway, the husband is to *protect* his family. And if the interaction of diverse personalities is confusing and disruptive, the husband is to be the correlator, the coordinator, the unifier. That is, in a role something like a parking attendant directing cars, he is to *preside.*

All this ensures a proper refuge, a safe haven. But the wife makes the haven worth all the trouble. She *nurtures* those who gather there.

It turns out these roles are not exclusive. Eve's primary role is nurturing, but she also helps Adam in his primary role of providing, protecting, and presiding because he cannot really do all this entirely on his own. His secondary role, in turn, is to support Eve in her enormous and unrelenting task to nurture. With her help, he hews, hefts, and hauls materials to the doorway. With his help, she refines, combines, and beautifies those materials. This is cooperation but much more. It is a harmony of consecration.

Both creators—the nurturer on one hand and the provider-protector-presider on the other—consecrate their all to a mission bigger than one person. Each is committed to the other person's role, the other person's powers, and the other person's needs. Our individual roles are avenues of mutual love.

Marriage is a special case, different from other human relations. Each partner is thoroughly involved in the other's life and each is partly responsible for how the other feels, sharing burdens that are normally considered personal. The husband is largely focused on his wife, her sense of safety, her assurance that she is beautiful and cherished (Ephesians 5:23). She, on the other hand, knows that she is essential to his peace and comfort. Tough as he would like to be, she knows that he really does need comforting, or the Lord would not have suggested it (D&C 25:5).

Very quiet, sacred feelings sometimes urge us to improve our part of the companionship. These are micro-nudges from the Holy Ghost, an expert on the subject of being a good and comforting companion. If we heed his patient example and gentle counsel, certainly we will be a delightful marriage partner.

Notes

1. *Teachings of the Prophet Joseph Smith,* sel. Joseph Fielding Smith (Salt Lake City: Deseret Book, 1976), 157–58.
2. "The Family—A Proclamation to the World," *Ensign,* November 1995, 102.

Chapter 21

THE LOFTY SOUL OF WOMAN

The true spirit of The Church of Jesus Christ of Latter-day Saints gives to woman the highest place of honor in human life (The First Presidency).[1]

The gospel of Jesus Christ . . . teaches the highest respect for woman that may be described by human speech or wrought into practice (B. H. Roberts).[2]

Anyone who questions the worth or equality of woman is certainly not taking clues from the prophets. And as for what the revelations say about men, the clues suggest that they need some work. In any case it is safe to say that man, through his callings in the home and in the Church, may get the training and growth he needs in order to stand next to his wife in eternity.

Gender is an essential characteristic of individual premortal, mortal, and eternal identity and purpose (The First Presidency and the Council of the Twelve Apostles).[3]

In our preparations for earth life, the "sisters received special gifts" (Russell M. Nelson).[4] No doubt, both men and women were given much more than a body type to match their identity. Our gender roles called for powers and inclinations to be wired into our spirit selves, blended with heart and mind. These had to be developed, as any gift must be, with time and effort long before we took up physical bodies.

> *Feminine characteristics are an endowment from God. . . . Women of God, both old and young, are spiritual and sensitive, tender and gentle. They have a kind, nurturing nature. This is your inheritance. . . . Develop the divinity that is within you (Margaret D. Nadauld).*[5]

It appears that all of us, both men and women, come here only partly developed. We need to keep growing.

> *Woman is God's supreme creation. . . . There is none more beautiful, none more inspiring than a lovely daughter of God who walks in virtue . . . and constantly enlarges the horizon of her understanding, who nurtures her spirit with everlasting truth (Gordon B. Hinckley).*[6]

One of the lessons of Church history is that women, who have so much capacity to labor for the kingdom in other ways, are generally allowed to remain at their more important post: the home. We notice, for example, that Emma Smith was preeminently qualified to be a scribe to the Prophet in the translation of the Book of Mormon. In fact, Emma served in this way briefly, long enough to become acquainted firsthand with the miraculous process. It would have been convenient for her to continue serving this way through the completion of the project.

In the long view, the kingdom is the means, whereas the family is the end. The keeping of a home, even for the smallest family in the smallest cabin, is a holy work, and for Emma there was plenty to do before sundown each day. Others would be raised up to assist Joseph in his work outside the home. It was not Emma's lot to be a subordinate to her husband. The most important book in the world was at stake. We might claim that bringing Martin Harris and later Oliver Cowdery into the project was extremely inconvenient. But God chose not to draw a young wife away from her sacred role, nor away from her equal standing with her husband in their home, especially at this time of setting patterns for millions of other couples. A little home ranks right up there with a volume of scripture.

No wonder, then, the Lord has declared that "women have claim on their husbands for their maintenance" (D&C 83:2). The ideal, the divine pattern, is that a wife has quite enough resting upon her shoulders without having to be a provider also.

On the other hand, patterns are not made of iron. The Lord himself sometimes calls for a departure, as when Emma temporarily served as scribe. Departures try the patience of covenant husbands and wives who long for the pattern. They pray and plan for circumstances that will permit them to enjoy their ideal and rightful roles. Those prayers will be answered in due time. But in the meantime, their faith helps them remember that departures are just departures and that greater joys await them when the departure is past.

Departure or not, it usually turns out that women do more than their share. Great burdens often befall lofty beings.

> *Woman. . . . has borne more than half the burdens, she has made more than half the sacrifices, she has suffered the most of the heartaches and sorrows (J. Reuben Clark Jr.).*[7]

Notes

1. In *Messages of the First Presidency of The Church of Jesus Christ of Latter-day Saints,* comp. James R. Clark, 6 vols. (Salt Lake City: Bookcraft, 1965–75), 6:5, 133.

2. *Defense of the Faith and the Saints,* 2 vols. (Salt Lake City: Deseret News, 1907), 2:436.
3. "The Family—A Proclamation to the World," *Ensign,* November 1995, 102.
4. "How Firm Our Foundation," *Ensign,* May 2002, 75.
5. "Hold High the Torch," *Ensign,* May 2002, 96.
6. "Our Responsibility to Our Young Women," *Ensign,* September 1988, 11.
7. In Conference Reports of The Church of Jesus Christ of Latter-day Saints (Salt Lake City: The Church of Jesus Christ of Latter-day Saints, April 1940), 21.

Chapter 22

The Blessing Role of Man

The priesthood . . . is not a passive power. Brethren, be generous with the power of blessing which comes through the priesthood. . . . Remember that the Lord has said, "Whomsoever you bless I will bless" (James E. Faust).[1]

If the husband's work—providing, protecting, presiding—could be boiled down to one word, it might be "blessing." To bless is the work of the priesthood in time and eternity. It is the chief business of the Eternal Father himself (Moses 1:39; 6:47; 7:35). When a man is not sure what else to do, it is a good policy to bless.

It is unrighteous exercise of priesthood authority for a man, as a conduit through his priesthood office, to withhold or limit blessings that should flow through the priesthood to his wife and family (James E. Faust).[2]

A man has little need for power if he is not in the blessing business. Humility in the male role consists in taking that business seriously and inviting a power above himself. That power seldom comes down without an invitation being offered up first.

Fortunately, priesthood is bigger than the man who holds it. It introduces the presence of God into human situations (D&C 84:20). The conduit of priesthood light is intended to bless others rather than the priesthood holder himself. He is the receptacle rather than the recipient, the servant rather than the served. He holds the power for the benefit of others, not for himself. This outlook, the attitude of a servant, is a key to genuine providing, protecting, and presiding.

At the close of his forty-day fast, Jesus had no food at hand. "That should be no problem," Satan seemed to say. "If you really are what you think you are, you ought to be able to turn these stones into bread" (Matthew 4:2–3). The devil was counseling the Great Jehovah! His counsel was wrong as usual. Jesus, who is the very source of priesthood power, knew what Satan has never accepted: The power entrusted to a man is for blessing but not for blessing himself.

> *The superior power that Jesus possessed had not been given to Him for personal gratification, but for service to others. . . . Though by miracle such a one might be fed, the miraculous supply would have to be given, not provided by himself. . . . [Satan] utterly failed in his attempt to induce Jesus to use His inherent power for personal service (James E. Talmage).*[3]

When a priesthood holder needs a blessing, he may go to God or to some other person holding God's authority. He does not lay his hands on his own head; he does not use this magnificent power in his own service. Natural, down-to-earth powers might be focused on personal gain or pleasure, but the priesthood man uses them to fulfill his mission.

The priesthood is an unseen robe of pure unselfishness. But a man cannot slip in and out of it. What is true of the priesthood he holds must also be true of him, all the time. He is to be first in line to help, last in line to be served (Mark 10:42–45; D&C 50:26).

The sacred conduit of light is not to pass *around* the priesthood man. He must be pure so that it may pass *through*, unobstructed. Priesthood is pointless without purity, and the purity must come first. A man's right to control what is outside himself is based on his control of what is inside himself (D&C 50:27–28; 121:36).

> *When a man accepts the Priesthood, he accepts the obligation of controlling himself under any circumstances (David O. McKay).*[4]

There is no way to be a real man in any other way. The Ultimate Man—the Man who sets the standard for all males—is, after all, a Man of Holiness and nothing less (3 Nephi 27:27; Moses 7:35).

A little boy explores his boundaries of pain and tussles with opposition. Some of this exploration is actual, while some of it is vividly imagined. But to him it is quite real. He investigates power in some form or perhaps in several forms. These childish explorations are crucial lessons. Instinctively and awkwardly, he tests and primes himself for his role to powerfully provide, protect, and preside.

Eventually, the boy's imaginary adventures are replaced by real ones. His skirmishes with evil are no longer pretended. The small fascinations that once trained his mind finally give way to bigger things. To the man with an honest heart, there comes the miracle of growing up. Finally, and reluctantly in the case of some, the time comes to "put away childish things" (1 Corinthians 13:11).

> *For a man to be great, he must not dwell on small things, though he may enjoy them (Joseph Smith).*[5]

Those small things are not necessarily evil by their nature. But if a man is to be in the blessing business, he cannot afford to *dwell* on them. Now and then he is given invitations to move ahead, to dwell on bigger things, to grow up. These are usually whisperings in his depth, so quiet that they leave him a free choice about walking through the door of growth. Little distractions, or perhaps pernicious addictions, offer him another option: he can just as easily hesitate, halt, and hang back from his destination. He can remain small, trifling with matters that do not matter, clinging to his lesser self. Or he can take the next step, make the change, accept the invitation.

The Sabbath is a recurring intersection in the path of growing up, a special chamber for hearing those whispers. Every seventh day, the man revisits his covenant in a sacred meeting called by God himself. Sacrament time bids a man to wonder what refinement should come next. The honest husband accepts the invitation to take another step toward his destiny as a family leader.

Notes

1. "I Believe I Can, I Knew I Could," *Ensign,* November 2002, 52.
2. In *Love* (Salt Lake City: Deseret Book, 1986), 14.
3. *Jesus the Christ* (Salt Lake City: The Church of Jesus Christ of Latter-day Saints, 1981), 121–22.
4. In Conference Reports of The Church of Jesus Christ of Latter-day Saints (Salt Lake City: The Church of Jesus Christ of Latter-day Saints, October 1958), 87.
5. *History of The Church of Jesus Christ of Latter-day Saints,* ed. B H. Roberts, 7 vols., 2d ed. rev. (Salt Lake City: The Church of Jesus Christ of Latter-day Saints, 1932–51), 5:298.

Chapter 23

INFLUENCING SOULS

To provide and protect, one must influence *things*. But presiding is more demanding still, for it is the influencing of *souls*. This influence is leadership but not domination, authority without a heavy hand, inspiration without manipulation. It is shaping without shoving, affecting without pressuring, guiding without goading. Does this sound like the work of a God? It is.

> *Fatherhood is leadership, the most important kind of leadership. . . . It is your place to give direction relating to all of family life (The Quorum of the Twelve Apostles).*[1]

To lead literally means to draw or extend, to bring something or someone along. To do this in God's way, there can be no yanking or yelling. All things testify not only of the existence of God but of his patience. To draw his children toward their greatest possibilities, without coercion, is almost never a quick job. Usually, it takes a lifetime. Many a good person, after years of success during business hours, has been astonished at the perplexing, soul-stretching difficulty of being a good leader to just one little child.

Since there are so many ways for a man to preside poorly, it takes some care to get it right. It may mean studying the live demonstrations that come along every now and then. The Lord's anointed, for example, are called because of their ways and their words. In addition, we can study the example of the Anointed One himself. The covenant specifies that we "always remember" this leader of all leaders (D&C 20:77, 79). One thing worth remembering about him day in and day out is the way he influences others—the way he presides.

Jesus cannot always delegate his godly tasks. But whenever he can, he does (JST, John 4:3–4; John 14:12). One form of unrighteous dominion is the buffoonery of a one-man show, which is especially absurd in a marriage. At home, an amateur duet is infinitely better than a professional solo. "Leading" without unity is silly. Since all of us are still learning how to lead, well-meaning silliness abounds (D&C 121:39).

> *You have a wife—a companion, a counselor, a partner, a helpmeet, a friend. . . . Do you exercise righteous leadership with her? (The Quorum of the Twelve Apostles).*[2]

Lead *with her,* the living prophets have said, not *without her* or *in spite of her* or *over her.* The husband works at being caring rather than charismatic. He is not the boss but rather the appointed representative of his marriage. He is the agent for a united council.

The best decisions are creations made unitedly in council under the spirit of inspiration.[3] A person is not a council, but a council can be much like a person—a *super*person.

> *A man who holds the priesthood accepts his wife as a partner in the leadership of the home and family with full knowledge of and full participation in all decisions relating thereto. . . . For a man to operate independent of or without regard to the feelings and counsel of his wife in governing the family is to exercise unrighteous dominion (Howard W. Hunter).*[4]

Only a unanimous council is entitled to the blessings of heaven (D&C 107:27–31). In council, neither husband nor wife is primary, and neither is secondary. The husband tries never to offend the very purpose of their council by dominating the time. He makes sure that it meets often, protects it from interruption, and hopes his partner will speak freely. As any good leader, he refrains from simply announcing or imposing a decision. Instead, he summons light from the mind of his partner. He is not trying to imitate the loud or self-centered leaders so common in the world. His hero is the King who loves to empower others.

> *Is yours a culture where the husband exerts a domineering, authoritarian role, making all of the important decisions for the family? That pattern needs to be tempered so that both husband and wife act as equal partners, making decisions in unity (Richard G. Scott).*[5]

The leader-husband listens for the voice of God in the counsel of his companion. He listens and listens again. He senses when two minds are becoming one, and he is fully aware when they are not. When this little eternal organization reaches a wise and united decision, he exercises faith and goes to work so that the will of the council may come to pass.

A partner is an equal and nothing less. No one is quite so entitled to sense the best direction for a man's life as his wife. Eve offered her husband the fruit of the tree of knowledge, Adam accepted her offer, and one of the wisest decisions in human history was made (Moses 4:12). When a man of the gospel covenant honors his wife as a source of wisdom, that is just what she becomes.

Notes

1. "Father, Consider Your Ways," *Ensign,* June 2002, 16.
2. Ibid., 15.
3. M. Russell Ballard, *Counseling with Our Councils: Learning to Minister Together in the Church and in the Family* (Salt Lake City: Deseret Book, 1997), 1–20.
4. "Being a Righteous Husband and Father," *Ensign,* November 1994, 50–51.
5. "Removing Barriers to Happiness," *Ensign,* May 1998, 86.

Chapter 24

GLIMPSES

HE WILL KEEP HIS PROMISES

The following was written by a man of faith who several years ago found himself reeling from an unexpected divorce.

> In my childhood, I had a wonderful, comforting feeling as I attended Church meetings and activities. This was partly because I felt so secure to be on the path to happiness: graduate from Primary, receive the Aaronic Priesthood, attend seminary, advance to the Melchizedek Priesthood, attend institute, serve a mission, graduate from institute and college, marry in the temple, and live happily ever after.
>
> As I traveled this path, somewhere along the way my marriage failed. After twenty-four years of family home evenings, temple trips, general conferences, home teaching, education weeks, and more, my marriage ended. I could not believe it was possible. I searched and searched my memory for some priesthood or gospel doctrine lesson on what to do when a long-term relationship evaporates into thin air and your life is changed forever. I drew a blank. We had prepared for famine, earthquake, unemployment, and war but not divorce. It shook my belief system to the very foundation.

At one point the Evil One reasoned with me that God does not keep his promises to his children even if they have served him over the years. I had no evidence in that state of mind to refute these claims. I could feel my testimony crumbling like a sandcastle. The emotional and spiritual trauma were indescribable.

Instinctively I went to my bishop, who immediately saw that something was wrong. He placed his hands upon my head and gave me a blessing that reached all the way to the deepest chambers of my heart.

When I was in such desperate need of reassurance, the Spirit bore witness to me that my Heavenly Father would still keep all his promises to me. It was up to me to just continue keeping my promises to him. So I work hard at doing that. I am still single, but I'm not alone.

We have been told that approximately one-third of the members of the Church over eighteen are single. Many converts who join the Church each year are also single. Yes, we are and always will be a family church—God's family. I realize now that he is brooding over the happiness of each one of us regardless of marital status. I believe the words we sing, "Fear not, I am with thee; oh be not dismayed, . . . I'll strengthen thee, help thee, and cause thee to stand."[1]

I have been supported and sustained . . . by the Church, its leaders, my friends, and the continuing assurances of the Holy Ghost . . . through every condition and heartache. By these helps, Heavenly Father has stayed by me. I know he will be with me the rest of the way. I know he will eventually grant whatever blessing I happen to be missing right now.

I JUST HAVE TO BE TRUE

The woman who wrote the following has been faithful since childhood. But her husband wandered, disaster struck her marriage, and divorce extinguished the fire she had relied on for many years. She experienced a cold loneliness and heartache she had never known. Through all the upheaval, one thing did not change: she remained true to the Lord in the gospel covenant. She is determined that this one thing will remain the same forever.

> For more than twenty years of marriage, the idea of divorce never entered my mind. I understood that if two people loved the Lord and loved each other they could stay together. But what I had not considered was what could happen if one of those marriage companions ceased to love the Lord. And when my husband no longer loved me or was kind to me, my love for him could not change his heart or his direction.
>
> It has been three years since the divorce. In that time I have heard stories about the various ways people are tested in these terrible situations. In my own case, the test was not about forgiving my husband or feeling anger toward the Lord. It had to do with my own feelings of worth. Simply put, I believed that I was unlovable. I believed that a man could not fall in love with me and maintain that love.
>
> In combination with my sense of failure, my feelings of being unlovable and the constant emotional and verbal abuse during the last two years of marriage had made me a mess. I was vulnerable.

Sometimes I didn't think clearly about everything. I was in a spiritual danger zone. Before I got back to feeling "normal" again, there were tests. I began to see that it wouldn't be hard to find "love" in a worldly way.

But at the same time, I never forgot the main thing: years earlier I had gone down into the baptismal waters and made a promise to a real, living God. I had gone into his temple and made promises. I had renewed my covenants hundreds of times in sacrament meetings. So I stayed on that path. I kept serving in the Church, attending the temple, and holding home evenings with my children. With a different view than I had ever had before, I studied the scriptures, and they opened up in new ways.

I prayed, often in tears, that my effort would someday take me out of the sorrow that seemed to follow me around. I hoped that my insecurity was only a temporary illness that could be healed. I hoped that someday a worthy and good man could love me, though it was hard to imagine.

The distress in my heart decreased but very gradually. It seemed that during times of confusion or when tempted to give up, some "messenger" would come along, some friend or leader would share with me just the right words, or I would hear just the right story from someone's mistake, and it would act as a warning. When faced with moments of truth, I always had just enough strength to do the right thing. It seems that strength usually isn't granted until it's needed.

Now, after three years, I am not as emotional, my thinking is clear, and I'm not as needy. I'm still lonely, but it doesn't hurt anymore. Of course there will be more tests. But a miracle has taken place, a miracle that was supporting me all along. Through all of this, I somehow know that I will someday have a wonderful companion, though I can't say when it will be or even whether it will be in this life. That doesn't matter to me as much now. The Lord will take care of things. I just have to be true to him.

IMPRESSIONS FROM A GARDEN

One summer I took a few of my children on a car trip to Nauvoo, Illinois. I had hoped we could arrive in time to visit something exciting and historic before finding our hotel room. But it was late when we pulled into town, and all the sites were closed and dark.

We drove to the visitors' center and walked around, gazing through the glass of the locked doors. "Too bad," I thought. "Oh well, we might as well take a walk through the one lighted spot available." Behind the center was a memorial garden dedicated to the Relief Society and to womankind in general.

There, enclosed in gently sweeping masonry and verdant foliage, we walked among the statues depicting woman's several roles and relationships. My children seemed to be content to browse and converse quietly during the next hour, a diversion from the long day on car seats. My own experience that night was one never to be forgotten.

Instead of a connection with the nineteenth century, I found myself somehow aware of eternal things. It occurred to me that, in addition to the latter-day restoration of priesthood, there had been a latter-day completion of womanhood—the bright return of a long-buried understanding of feminine dignity and holiness.

For several days afterward, my mind continued to rest upon the partnership I had with my own precious wife, who was hundreds of miles away hoping we were having a good trip. I saw her gifts in a new way. She had managed to use them to fashion gifts for us—gifts of fire, light, and warmth suited to each of us in different ways. Such thoughts awakened me to the heritage of women in my lineage, the beauty and innocence of my daughters, and the heritage to be transferred through their unselfishness to an endless future of queenly descendants. I frequently found a lump in my throat as I realized that preceding all this was the supernal prototype of gracious womanhood, the Eternal Mother.

That picture of womanhood is refreshed and expanded now and then, and I ask again, "How could I have missed it before?" But I know the answer. We live in a world influenced by Satan. To him it is imperative that neither men nor women understand the truth about women. Satan's cardboard stage is designed to repudiate the restoration of truth. He works around the clock to degrade the women who once rejected his fraudulent plan.

I often think of that night in Nauvoo when I see the sisters in Church meetings. Some sit alone for one reason or another. Others try to pay attention while retrieving broken Cheerios from the hymnbook rack. Some have arms that ache for a child, but they go forward with sweet dignity, patiently awaiting the due time of the Lord. At times two or three of them, arms aching with a heavy, groggy infant, sway from side to side in the back of the chapel. Each has her own quiet, wonderful way of erasing the world's picture and restoring the truth about womanhood.

Note

1. *Hymns of The Church of Jesus Christ of Latter-day Saints* (Salt Lake City: The Church of Jesus Christ of Latter-day Saints, 1985), no. 85.

Joined by Children

We are joined by our children in more than one sense. Obviously, they join us in the sense of coming from another world into ours. They enlist in our cause, add their lives to the mix, spice up the recipe of a home atmosphere, and make our adventures a lot more interesting!

But children also have the power to join a man and a woman to each other. The attraction that creates a baby is usually not as strong as the bond that draws parents together when they focus on a child's worth and growth long after birth. Once we devote ourselves to the maturity and salvation of our children, our marital conversations and covenants and our cares and prayers are never the same again. Our children give us new reasons to be close, to pull in the same direction, and to pull with all our might. They not only help join us to each other but also to our God.

And this life is only the beginning of our parental privileges. Millions of valiant souls, whose precious bodies were laid to rest in childhood, will be resurrected with celestial glory in the great Millennium, and many of these will need righteous parents. Wondrous surprises are reserved in that day for those who now long for offspring. And, of course, exaltation will be marked by the privilege of bringing forth life forever. Thus President Brigham Young spoke this assurance:

> *Many of the sisters grieve because they are not blessed with offspring. You will see the time when you will have millions of children around you. If you are faithful to your covenants, you will be mothers of nations.*[1]

Chapter 25

Mothers as Angels

You know all women are good, or ought to be. They were made for angelic beings. . . . Man is made of rougher material, to open the way, cut down bushes, and kill the snakes, that women may walk along through life, and not soil and tear their skirts (Heber C. Kimball).[2]

A father is responsible for what we might call "ways and means." Even when the mother is a bit more qualified to do this, she simply cannot afford to do everything. To be "angelic" requires focus. The ideal is that every home will have its man and its angel and that the man will do what he can to liberate his angel for her ministry.

One thing this world does not seem to need more of is women who have allowed themselves to become self-absorbed or faithless. If the angels in our lives lose their ability to lift hearts, the world sinks (Isaiah 3:16, 25).

Beauty is one of the tools in a mother's hands for lifting her family. The world disables this tool by focusing almost all attention upon exterior appearance, leaving the impression that this is all there is. Mother has to be wise enough to see through this falsehood, for her convictions about beauty will have an enormous effect on her children and on their sense of wholeness.

The radiant and whole kind of beauty may end up public, but it starts out in private. It is the fruit of living in a manner that befits our original home. Unto woman is given the charge for inspiring it in all of us. What makes a wife and mother exquisitely beautiful is the modesty that prompts her to draw attention to other beauty besides her own.

Adam held the priesthood, and Eve served in matriarchal partnership with the patriarchal priesthood (Russell M. Nelson).[3]

As a nurturing angel, a mother adds strength to the priesthood when she strengthens the father in the home. Her relationship with the priesthood is one of equality and partnership. Her husband affiliates with divine authority through those "up the line" from him. But for her, the priesthood touches her life, not through an officer above but through an equal at her side. It is a lesson her sons and daughters will probably not see anywhere else.

Though she places herself in her husband's care—honoring his calling to provide and protect—a mother's special kind of submissiveness is different from other kinds. It is "not afraid with any amazement" as the Apostle Peter said of Sarah's relationship with Abraham (1 Peter 3:5–6). Sarah felt neither threatened nor outranked, neither fear nor inferior.

By an act of faith, a mother sustains and inspires as any good angel would do with imperfect people. Her willingness to let an equal—her husband—preside rests calmly on her belief in the plan of family life. Likewise, she may spend a majority of her waking hours with immature minds and undeveloped personalities instead of with interesting adults. She cheerfully realizes that time so spent will yield the greater return. Such cheer will stay in the minds of her loved ones long after her labors are finished.

Consider how important her confidence is to her husband's leadership. A husband cannot really preside unless his wife lets him! Her choice to let him preside is made without constraint, or else it is no choice at all. He, in turn, has to let her freely make that decision. This is much like the proposal of marriage: he makes a proposal, and she decides whether to accept it. Only she can determine whether this man will preside in their home and whether she will enable him to magnify life's other important callings. He has to let go of the question, for it is chiefly her business.

On close inspection, we notice something very important about this permission the wife gives her husband: her approach will dramatically affect the way her children accept or sustain the leadership of their father. The day will very likely come when his influence upon them will depend on her maturity in letting him preside.

Through faithfulness, every woman is a candidate to "bear the souls of men" as a glorified and transcendent mother in eternity (D&C 132:63). Her candidacy begins with her own earthly infancy. A tiny baby girl born to bring forth life? Yes. It is the Father's plan. In fact, her preparations began while still living with her Eternal Mother.

The enemy keeps trying to derail her career after she becomes a mother if he cannot do so before. He hopes she will be fascinated with anything except that covenant path that leads straight into worlds of infinite light. In matters of spending or earning, bearing or rearing, working or worshipping, at every important intersection, she has to keep her eye on eternity. It seems that questions keep coming up, and every day brings another choice between the covenant and a bowl of pottage (Genesis 25:29–34).

Mother—and all of us who inhabit her world—should know that there is no one in creation more splendid, more full of possibilities, more important to myriad beings yet unborn than a woman who is willing to be an angel to her family.

Notes

1. In *Journal of Discourses,* 26 vols. (London: Latter-day Saints' Book Depot, 1854–86), 8:208.
2. Ibid., 2:154.
3. *The Power Within Us* (Salt Lake City: Deseret Book, 1988), 109.

Chapter 26

FATHERS AS "TREASURERS"

The bills contracted by the family are payable by the head, the provider. The root of the word *head* means to lift or carry.[1] Over time, *head* came to mean the topmost part. The father has to be on top of things, not so that he might be honored but so that he might be helpful. He uses his contact with the heavens to carry out his constant business of blessing. The head moves ahead in matters of repentance and worthiness, else what good is he to the family? Let him lay the track, break the trails, find a way through to the light. And if anyone in a particular family must bear humiliation or trouble, let it be the head.

Associated with the principle of a family provider, therefore, is the principle of atonement—covering the household debts. This proxy work is a male role, featured clearly in the plan of salvation.

> *If any man of you bring an offering unto the Lord, . . . let him offer a male without blemish (Leviticus 1:2–3).*

Similarly, the family head protects. Let the husband survey the dangers and turn away the enemy at the gate. Think of Captain Moroni, whose wartime firmness was preceded by another kind of heroism during days of peace. No doubt he had to face a certain amount of public criticism for doing so, but Moroni so courageously "altered the management of affairs" among his people that the enemy could not easily prey upon them in case of war (Alma 49:11). Some must have felt that his tendency to "labor exceedingly for the welfare and safety of his people" was uncalled for (Alma 48:12). But in hindsight we now know that he saved an entire covenant race.

If all family heads provided and protected with this sort of firmness against the subtle and aggressive influence of evil, what influence could evil ever have? (Alma 48:17). In our day of extreme jeopardy, the family needs a father on the job.

Even the Son of God, the greatest of all, needed a mortal man to watch and teach him while he was young. That life was destined to surmount untold odds, but this in no way suggested that he should begin his mortal life without a man nearby. Even the simplest and tiniest human knows that every child deserves a feminine mother and a masculine father.

Beyond being the treasure provider and treasure protector of the family, the father must know what the *real* treasure is. He must not be confused about what to cherish most.

It is easy to bless what we treasure. The key, then, is for a man to realize that his family, his wife foremost of all, *is* his treasure. If he does so, respect and courtesy will come more naturally. He will more readily send away every muttering complaint that sneaks up on his mind or his lips. His coarseness will give way to the manner of Christ.

The father who is not sure what "courtesy" means can remember its root: to "court." Courting his wife and courting the good will of his children is a never-ending privilege. The word *respect*—to see again or look carefully, to see with our second eyes, to see with our heart—also teaches a lesson. Like the Lord, the wise father, instead of looking upon the outward appearance, "looketh upon the heart" (1 Samuel 16:7). If he is pure, he may have this gift of localized "seership," this special kind of sight, within the realm of his special little world, his home.

Every wife wants to be married to her own personal gentle-man who delights her. Every child is entitled to live in a home where the father honors the mother. So it was with Adam. We can picture him standing up whenever Eve came into his presence, finding flowers to give her, and addressing her in the noblest terms (Genesis 3:20; Moses 4:26). It is impossible to imagine a belittling tone. And where could Adam have inherited his gentle traits except from the Universal Gentleman, our Father?

Any man who demeans or belittles his wife affronts her Father in Heaven (Gordon B. Hinckley).[2]

One of the saddest facts in history is that some males have failed to bless and lead and treasure. We wish that no tender hearts had ever been broken by disloyal and unruly men. We would like to think that no trusting children had sobbed themselves to sleep because of untrustworthy fathers. But, in fact, "many hearts [have] died, pierced with deep wounds" (Jacob 2:35). When the innocent believe without reservation, nothing can so thoroughly break their hearts as a shattered trust. And when the sobbing subsides, usually it is scorn or rage that festers where trust once flourished.

The sons of God always have a mission to reverse this trend. An earth full of agony and disappointment cries out for males whose "faithfulness is stronger than the cords of death" (D&C 121:44). The world would be transformed if men were good treasurers.

And without question, that role can transform the man who fulfills it. The way he treasures his family is his response to the covenant. If his offering is clumsy or inconsistent, let him just do more homework. He will eventually get it right because he was created in the image of him who fills that male role to perfection.

God is a father and a marriage companion. It is our privilege to imitate him and thus come to understand his plan not only by doctrine but also by experience.

> *The day will come when you will stand before the Lord and report your stewardship as a father on earth. Father, consider your ways. What will be your report? (The Quorum of the Twelve Apostles).*[3]

All future moments in an endless train of ages will be affected by that report. So this is the hour of hours. Nothing a man does here can influence the rest of eternity so completely as his choice of treasure.

Notes

1. *Noah Webster's First Edition of an American Dictionary of the English Language* (1828; republished in facsimile, San Francisco: Foundation for American Christian Education, 1967), s.v. "head."
2. *Teachings of Gordon B. Hinckley* (Salt Lake City: Deseret Book, 1997), 322.
3. "Father, Consider Your Ways," *Ensign,* June 2002, 16.

Chapter 27

THE ENORMOUS LIFE OF A CHILD

It happens to Alice during her trip through Wonderland and to a number of other characters in fantasy literature. They endure one of the most humbling of experiences: they actually become little.

This is not just fantasy. The Father's plan required us to be downsized just as we left his presence. You might say he shrunk the kids. This is lucky for the mother during delivery, but a constant work of care follows. After all, babies come not only tiny but also helpless. Someone—two grown persons, in fact—will have to give up the majority of their waking hours to host the new arrival. Fortunately, it is worth it (Psalm 127:3).

Wrapped in all this frailty, appearing to be only a baby boy, is a giant with a royal history. The infant girl, meanwhile, is really a noble person from the deep past with promises to keep. Though it happens all the time, there is nothing commonplace about the arrival of such beings.

By putting these souls into our arms, God in no way releases himself as their Father. This is not the end to one relationship but the beginning of an added one. We easily forget that this child was and always will be God's. Once enjoying a gift, we sometimes take over, thinking it to be ours alone. For example, earthly parents are sometimes embittered at the death of a child, forgetting the tender, long-standing tie between the child and the original Eternal Parents.

We receive our child with an obligation to those original Parents. We are to raise that little one on their terms.

Little children are whole, for they are not capable of committing sin (Moroni 8:8; Moses 6:54).

When parents fail to teach a child of its divine origin, when their behavior deprives a child of divine dignity, or when they hamper a child in fulfilling a divine mission, those parents shrink their child's life in the wrong ways.

The way I treat a child—in public and private, in good moods and in bad moods—says very little about the child. Rather, it shows my reaction to that unvarnished kind of innocence that is "blameless before God" (Mosiah 3:21). The way I treat a child says everything about me and what I am.

He that supposeth that little children need baptism is in the gall of bitterness and in the bonds of iniquity; . . . wherefore, should he be cut off while in the thought, he must go down to hell (Moroni 8:14).

To hold in the mind the idea that an innocent person should be blamed, criticized, or punished is not an innocent thought. It is a rejection of too much good. It denies too many basics, including the Atonement itself. A lot of remodeling must be done on a viewpoint that looks at goodness and sees guilt. One with such convictions "must go down to hell," where evil views are revised, because there is simply nowhere else to go.

The innocent around us are the closest thing we have to royalty, to deity (Mormon 8:8, 12; Mosiah 3:18). They are, in this world, the only real celebrities. The vast spiritual component of the real universe is deeded to them because of their consummate purity.

One of the dangers in treating children—or any innocent person—as if they were fundamentally bad is that they might actually believe it, which is even more likely if they are younger and smaller than their accuser. It is too easy to crush natural good cheer and quench the small flames of hope that spring up spontaneously in a young heart.

But whoso shall offend one of these little ones which believe in me, it were better for him that a millstone were hanged about his neck, and that he were drowned in the depth of the sea (Matthew 18:6).

The character of a child unfolds about as slowly as the physical body matures. During the early months and years, teaching and affection have a colossal effect on the spiritual powers that will later emerge. The young know this too deeply to express.

While the body matures automatically, character needs coaching. For example, it is by character rather than by physical maturity that we are able to resist temptation, see an uninteresting job through to completion, face big disappointments without anger or blaming, sit still long enough to communicate with a loved one or with God, receive correction, or admit a big mistake. These powers are not doodads out of a toolbox. They are deep tissues, large muscle masses of the spirit polished by consistent exercise over a stretch of time. They were first shaped at our ease in the long ages of premortal life, but we come here to make them permanent in the fires of extremity. So the life of a little child is anything but little. It is enormous, and so is the opportunity to be on hand, influencing that child while the clay is soft.

Behold your little ones (3 Nephi 17:23).

To behold them is to hold them with reverence, keeping them in our care and sight. It is to insist on the gift of parental bias, cleaving to the vision of their worth so that their promise may be fulfilled.

Chapter 28

INVITING YOUR FRIENDS HOME

Of all the joys of life, none other equals that of happy parenthood (Gordon B. Hinckley).[1]

In this world there is a lot of emphasis on things of no consequence. But children can put us in touch with big matters. They teach us what we taught our own parents when we were young. But they come as more than young teachers. They are future best friends.

When a baby arrives, this new mystery guest is, of necessity, greeted by a hostess. Even before birth, the new one feels the gratitude and gentle greetings of the mother. She is like a veil from which the child emerges freshly draped in holiness. She is the portal between very different worlds, the only possible entry. She "gives birth" in the highest sense of giving. Lying at the very gates of death, she opens the gate of birth, and this she does for a stranger, or rather, a friend long forgotten. The new entrant steps through to new powers and dramatic opportunities but only at a high and singular price paid by the one who will be known as Mother. She offers herself with an amount of understandable fear, but she does it. To our amazement, she may even do this again and again, knowingly, gladly.

Birth settles something within her spirit. It puts to rest a question, though she may be too modest, and others who partake of her offering may be too unknowing, to see it. *She is a hero*—genuine, unscripted, down-to-earth, not favored with flattering lights and music. She is unposturing, mostly unheralded, but ready for action. As we all know, men attain to this level of heroism less often than women. The only hope most men have for attaining heroic stature is in giving themselves entirely to their own role of providing, protecting, and presiding.

The hosting heroes—mother and father—meet their new arrival at the one-way portal and then find themselves on the job around-the-clock. Proper parenthood is a promise to be there forever for emergencies and ecstasies. The warning that this would increase Eve's discomfort was not only about birth and the months before; the "labor" continues and intensifies for a lifetime. And perhaps the promise that pregnancy and birth would increase her sorrow also applies to an increase in accompanying character that would come to her and her husband in their ensuing family adventures (Genesis 3:16).

When a couple invites an eternal being to become their child, they assume a commitment both wondrous and weighty. But to decline, to disinvite that child, to close the gate, is also weighty.

If the decision were only about that one child—whether to provide for, protect, nurture, and warmly associate with that one soul forever—it would be momentous enough. But that one, in the Father's covenant, is the ambassador of a future that cannot be imagined, generations that cannot be numbered. Upon deciding to enter the covenant, Rebekah's blessing was that she would be "the mother of thousands of millions" (Genesis 24:60). Without using such startling terms, other scriptures point to the same privilege in other ways, by speaking of "seed," "increase," and "eternal lives" (Psalm 115:14; Isaiah 44:3; 48:19; Ezekiel 36:37; 1 Nephi 12:1, 8; D&C 131:4; 132:24, 55). Of course, bringing forth children is about love, not numbers. A new life is to be sought out in love, welcomed and held with love.

I was conversing with a man on the train, and he remarked to me: "Why,

> *Mr. Smoot, I have one child, and I would not take a million dollars for it; but I would not give five cents for another." . . . Let us, my brethren and sisters, show to the world that we love children more than we do lapdogs (Reed Smoot).*[2]

Of course, lapdogs cost less than human souls. That is something to consider. On the other hand, like the decision to pay tithing, the financial commitment to raise a child rests on faith.

The makeup of a whole lineage awaits the faith, hopes, and interests of a covenant couple. Does the course of history take its bearings from this pair of untried and struggling mortals? Does this seem wise, giving so much influence to a blithe man and woman, perhaps carefree or perhaps careworn, probably young and uncertain in their opinions? It is wisdom of the highest order. It is the very plan, illustrated perfectly by Adam and Eve.

They had been commanded to have children. With pure hospitality they did so. The first couple opened the way for multitudes by opening their lives to whatever spirits stood next in line. This is the nature of the covenant, to do momentous things, to direct traffic at the major intersections of eternity.

The sealing power even *re*-directs traffic, for it can override a blood relationship. When civil adoption laws have been satisfied and the affected persons agree, the sealing power can assign a parent-child relationship where there was none before, and this new bond is everlasting. Thus God's great plan is not dependent upon physical kinship. What makes the difference at those crucial intersections is the covenant. To enter it is to accept the gifts of sacred history past. To honor it is to create sacred history future.

Notes

1. "Save the Children," *Ensign,* November 1994, 54.
2. In Conference Reports of The Church of Jesus Christ of Latter-day Saints (Salt Lake City: The Church of Jesus Christ of Latter-day Saints, April 1903), 54.

Chapter 29

A Day for Strong Souls

The Lord has chosen a small number of choice spirits of sons and daughters out of all the creations of God, who are to inherit this earth; and this company of choice spirits have been kept in the spirit world for six thousand years to come forth in the last days to stand in the flesh in this last dispensation (Wilford Woodruff).[1]

Special work calls for special workers (Jacob 5:61–62, 70). It is no surprise that "choice" beings—rare, carefully selected—are sent for this matchless time. Some come directly to covenant homes; others are expected to "take hold" of the covenant as "sons of the stranger" (Isaiah 56:6–7).

I envy these young people. . . . They will see marvelous things in the years that lie ahead. I have no doubt of it whatever. The Church will grow and grow and grow, and no force under the heavens can stop it (Gordon B. Hinckley).[2]

We can be grateful that, after all this time, those mighty ones are finally taking the field. By the special timing and placement of their birth, they are "called to make a difference in the world" (The First Presidency).[3]

You are our shining hope. . . . You will make a significant difference in the final outcome. . . . You are the last great counterforce against the evil that is engulfing the earth (Dean L. Larsen).[4]

The arrival of our children, the final "counterforce" against evil, is being watched by an old and heartless enemy. Satan cannot stop the work, but he has been known to stop some of the workers. Choice people are special targets, and young people are easy targets. These who are so choice and yet so young were called in heaven, but their mission is here, on his turf.

Satan is hunting for consent. Before he can govern another soul, he must get permission. Any kind of permission counts, even if his prey is distracted, pressured, or enticed, as young people often are. He just needs that fleeting "yes" to begin draping a victim in miserable chains (2 Nephi 1:23; Moses 7:26). The typical person of inexperience, craving novelty, is at a grave disadvantage (2 Nephi 28:21–22).

Even the strongest newcomers need support. Focus is the key to their success, and focus would be tricky here even without the amnesia (Luke 11:34; D&C 88:67–69; 121:34–35). Who will teach them to focus? And, after being "held back" for so long, from whom will they learn to *stop* holding back? Who will train them in the Lord's work? Who will be their companions in the face of temptation? Who will encourage them and then encourage them again? Who will bless these who were sent to bless the latter-day world? The answer is their parents, who have been given to them for that very purpose.

There is no need to be theatrical or sugary in giving courage to the young. Our optimism is based on simple truth. Despite dangers, the heaven that chose them really does stand by to help them; a brilliant future really does await. We, who are called to give them hope, look to them for *our* hope as well.

In the classic movie *Chariots of Fire,* Eric Little's speed was only an expression of the fire burning underneath his muscles and nerves, a fire of convictions that drove him to train boldly and run bravely. The committee that urged him to compete on the Sabbath sought to separate his running from his convictions. They would have broken the very force that made him the athlete he was.

I have a deep sympathy for the young people. . . . They are in a new world. . . . My quarrel shall not be with them so much as with conditions that they must meet (Melvin J. Ballard).[5]

Let us not be discouraged by the fire in our children. If it were not dangerously hot, it would have no value. It is not to be extinguished but explored, controlled, and harnessed. Childhood enthusiasm is a reservoir of light and zeal. We can offer our children opportunities to put their fire to work, and by example we can show them how. A chilly reaction on our part, on the other hand, will not help. Nor will a scalding heat of our own.

As arrows are in the hand of a mighty man; so are children. . . . Happy is the man that hath his quiver full of them (Psalm 127:4–5).

Why compare children to arrows? With patience and skill, the archer sends out his straight, beautifully crafted shafts. He reaches places far from his presence, perhaps with arrows of protection or even with swiftly borne messages. Likewise, parents have an influence beyond their family and home through the lives of offspring going out to serve.

Timing (restraining children until the right time) and aim (pointing in the right direction) are everything in both archery and parenting. Happy is the person who sends out strong, straight, well-directed shafts that go far, that serve and protect, and that carry good tidings.

Notes

1. In *The Teachings of Ezra Taft Benson* (Salt Lake City: Bookcraft, 1988), 555.
2. "Inspirational Thoughts," *Ensign,* August 2000, 5.
3. In *Aaronic Priesthood, Priest: Fulfilling Our Duty to God* (Salt Lake City: The Church of Jesus Christ of Latter-day Saints, 2001), 4.
4. "The Strength of the Kingdom Is Within," *Ensign,* November 1981, 26–27.
5. In Conference Reports of The Church of Jesus Christ of Latter-day Saints (Salt Lake City: The Church of Jesus Christ of Latter-day Saints, April 1929), 65.

Chapter 30

A Decade for Becoming Strong

Elder Robert D. Hales once described the first thirty years of mortal life in three stages: a decade of exploration, a decade of preparation, and a decade of decision. Of the third decade, when we are in our twenties, he said, "Just think . . . what decisions will be made."

> *Temple worthiness, missionary service, education, career, an eternal companion, and a family. This decade of decision is not a time to fear. It is a time to enjoy the blessings for which you have prepared. "If ye are prepared ye shall not fear" (Robert D. Hales).*[1]

The decade of preparation, from about ten to twenty years of age, is a time to *prepare* for eternal decisions (Alma 37:35). It is hard to imagine how any other ten-year period in eternity could be of greater importance.

Decisions emerge from character, and so this decade is for gaining character: learning to direct thoughts, channel desires, and tame feelings. The decade when our inner events seem to be most surprising and mutinous is the ideal time to take charge of them. But anyone who thinks this is easy has probably forgotten their teenage years.

> *This relationship of character to thought cannot be too strongly emphasized. How could a person possibly become what he is not thinking? (Spencer W. Kimball).*[2]

One of the most strategic things we will ever do is best done in that second decade of life—choosing the right things to think about.

Briefly try to imagine, or remember, what it is like to actually live in that decade of preparation. If you are a teenager, you have so many powers and perplexities emerging in you that these years may seem like one big emergency. What was obvious by pure instinct in childhood now seems to come up for reconsideration.

For example, how do you figure out whether you are worth anything? In a few years, you will see that your immeasurable soul needs no measuring. But in the meantime, you look for signals from shallow sources, which leads to the ridiculous habit of judging not only yourself but almost everyone else as well.

If you take your signals from the One who is a real expert on the subject of you, these problems rarely come up. If you really trust him, you can simply believe that you are precious and drop the whole question (D&C 18:10).

Mortal life is unavoidably physical. But in the teen years the physical is both new and intense. He who scheduled all this is certainly not offended by it. But he asks that we go about our adventures with respect and purity, keeping our promises to him and keeping our eye on him.

The physical body is connected with our emotions in countless ways. But during teen years, this wiring is in constant revision. Mother Nature seems to be saying, "Please excuse the mess. I am only remodeling your bones and muscles, your complexion and shape, the emotion center of your brain, the subtle features of your central nervous system, your hormones and your social powers in order to better serve you." Adolescents may feel as if emotions, like the weather, just "happen" to them.

If you are a teenager, you are strongly attracted to the smiles and personal interest of others. But some smiles of approval should be avoided at all costs. Not all friendships are as important as your emotions want them to be. The beacon that will lead you wisely, as Elijah learned, is not in the drama of wind, the swirl of fire, or the shudder of earth (1 Kings 19:11–12). The still voice never joins with the bizarre or showy or clever or loud. This you already suspect, but the second decade of your life is the time to learn it well. Just allowing yourself the luxury of some quiet, reverent time every day will make a huge difference.

> *I can taste the principles of eternal life, and so can you. . . . You are bound to receive them as sweet (Joseph Smith).*[3]

Newness may be exciting but not necessarily sweet. Those who are best at discerning between the really true and the merely new are the ones who have been tasting and obeying truth the longest (John 10:27; 14:6; 18:37; D&C 138:26). If you are young, you get to make that choice every day, for most things are new to you—important or not, true or not, helpful or not. Newness can lend enchantment to the useless, art to the crass, humor to the degrading. Strangely, novelty has been around for a long time. Most of it bores the devils and offends the angels.

If you are not a teenager, social interaction most likely ranks below 10 on a scale of 10. If you are a teenager, it is probably a 15! There are good reasons for this. We will enjoy "sociality"—being connected with other people—for eternity, and the adolescent years play a surprising part in getting us ready (D&C 132:2).

One of the healthiest teenagers in history, young Joseph Smith, longed for social contact. But he had problems. First, he was forbidden to join the local congregations. This limit on his social life was set by ironclad truth. In addition, Joseph was "of very tender years," when the human longing for friends makes a person vulnerable. Furthermore, Joseph was persecuted by people who should have been his friends. The religious youth in the Palmyra area were told that he was a villain, and they treated him accordingly. So, during rare hours away from his daily work, Joseph mixed in with the only people available, the boisterous and uninhibited laborers on the nearby canal. They no doubt enjoyed his manly and robust manner, his adventurous disposition and quick wit. Though he did not partake of their vices, he tells us:

> *I was left to all kinds of temptations; and mingling with all kinds of society, . . . displayed the weakness of youth (JS–H 1:28).*

Even if you are a teenager of faith, even if you have uncommon spiritual sensitivity, you are of "tender years." That means you need good friends, and your friendships during these years will affect your destiny.

Parents know these lessons. They may not any longer be of tender years, but they are expected to think back on what it was like to have, as Joseph Smith did, "the weakness of youth." They watch over the peculiar needs of their children with interest and compassion. Happy or sad, obedient or contrary, teenagers need at least a small handful of peers "to be [their] friends and [treat them] kindly" (JS–H 1:28).

To ignore these needs is to ask for trouble. Most good teenagers will not be quite so resilient as Joseph was in coping with the foibles of adolescence. He survived his loneliness without "any great or malignant sins" (JS–H 1:28), but what of your child or mine?

Wise parents will sympathize with their children during this leg of the journey and will help them get up the hills.

Notes

1. "Fulfilling Our Duty to God," *Ensign,* November 2001, 40.
2. *The Miracle of Forgiveness* (Salt Lake City: Bookcraft, 1969), 104.
3. *Teachings of the Prophet Joseph Smith,* sel. Joseph Fielding Smith (Salt Lake City: Deseret Book, 1976), 355.

Chapter 31

RAISING THE STRONG

He said there was a tender germ in every man which if rightly cultivated would [come] to be a God, . . . but it was very tender (Brigham Young).[1]

In Brigham Young's day, the word *germ* meant a seed or small beginning. God's own seed of divinity is planted in all of us and in all our children. The divinity is vast but the seed is vulnerable. As President Young warned, the beginning of a mighty being is "very tender." The delicate business of tending the tender seed is a cottage industry, a "Mom and Pop" business if there ever was one.[2] The secret is to go about it in the Lord's own way.

Strong spirits can be pretty unpredictable and ungainly while in development. The immature person needs to see and know maturity, up close, in a loved one. Young people cannot be what they do not know how to be. To expect that would be a step toward losing them. No good will come from being surprised or insulted by immaturity.

The Spirit of the Lord Omnipotent . . . has wrought a mighty change in us, or in our hearts, that we have no more disposition to do evil, but to do good continually (Mosiah 5:2; 27:25).

Mighty change comes on a divine schedule rather than on daily demand. Once the "disposition" or desire of a heart is altered and the direction in which a life is facing is corrected, the small changes can begin. Alien reflexes can break down—slowly. Old patterns give way to better ones—

slowly. The mighty change is contrary to old logic and long-held ideas, so these must be discerned, hunted down, and pried out of the thinking in a natural, unfolding sequence—but slowly. In other words, once the core has been transformed, the outer layers of habit and impulse gradually conform.

So as parents watch over the immature, they pray for the quickening power of God while they nurture the gradual, microscopic changes. They honor the enormous role that God has assigned to time.

Unrealistic demands guarantee distance, and endless advice guarantees anger. How can parents save at the same time they dispute? How will a parent's voice give hope or help if the child resents the sound of that voice? (Ephesians 6:4; Proverbs 15:1). By what desire might a child choose to walk in the path if the tour guides are cranky?

Someone around here has to be the adult. *Someone* has to invite Christ into the home. The divine duty to be a grown-up—to be emotionally and spiritually mature—belongs to the parent. The fathers are to be the first to turn their hearts; then the children can turn theirs (D&C 27:9; 128:17). To warmly restart the cycle over again each day calls for a full reservoir. This is why Jesus offered living water (John 4:10–14; 7:37–39). It takes a steady parent to be patient with an unsteady youth. But there is a Rock for that parent (Matthew 7:24–25).

If parents come unto the Father in private, they will be made equal to the job—a job they might actually enjoy! (Matthew 11:29–30). And though we must pay a price for our alliance with the most experienced Parent in the universe, we do not need to tell our children about that price. We just need to pay it.

Pray to thy Father which is in secret; and thy Father which seeth in secret shall reward thee openly. . . . When thou fastest, . . . appear not unto men to fast, but unto thy Father which is in secret: and thy Father, which seeth in secret, shall reward thee openly (Matthew 6:4, 6, 17–18).

Being a grown-up parent means believing that the Savior has a wise plan for each child. That plan requires us to see past any unflattering soil that has not yet been washed from the child's face and clothes. It is not denial of dark things that were but a confidence in bright things yet to be. Our belief empowers us to be patient—very patient and ever patient. It is the patient parent that can relax enough to radiate a healing hope instead of a toxic pessimism.

Our young ones will turn out more grown-up than we can imagine. We should remind ourselves that they have never been through this before, not in this world or in any other. So, obviously, they stumble.

We may bite our nails as we watch a child heft the unfamiliar mortal burden, but short nails are better than stunted souls. Our anxious or angry intrusions do nothing for their faith in the Lord, their confidence that the path really leads somewhere, or their desire to have us accompany them. Little children insist on dressing and feeding themselves for a good reason, and adolescents also have healthy instincts.

He had carried the griefs and the sorrows of my teenage heart, and through my obedience, He would continue to walk with me for the rest of my life (Sharon G. Larsen).[3]

That little glimpse was shared by a noble and queenly woman, but it was a glimpse of her "teenage heart" from years before. Even the good sometimes cry. She was a very good teenager, but she was still a teenager. She had the normal episodes of emotional pain. To her they were not small pains, and so they were not small to God either. Along with all the other sorrows of mankind, Christ carried her adolescent aches.

The Holy Ghost is sent to comfort, but parents do not have to let the Holy Ghost do all the comforting work alone. Mothers and fathers can listen and hold a hand, listen some more, and offer the smile of quiet confidence. They can help to soothe the young heart.

If we want the young to listen to us, we will first have to listen to them, at length—about their interests, on their terms, at their times. Most children need more ear and less lip. Listening, not talking, is the eloquent language of love.

Of course, there is a place for "reproof"—facing the truth about a personal fault. But this should come "betimes"—at just the right moment and only for a moment. The one giving reproof has a responsibility to show "an increase of love" soon afterward. If that is unfeasible, it is better to refrain from reproof altogether. It would be better to severely injure your own tongue in a biting accident than to leave anyone, especially your child, with reason to "esteem thee to be his enemy" (D&C 121:43).

Nagging or blaming does not resemble the frank and loving tone of "reproving betimes." It is just faultfinding, a habit that drives away the Spirit of God (D&C 88:124). Angry, contentious outbursts are really just invitations to host Satan in the home (Mosiah 2:32; 3 Nephi 11:29; D&C 10:63).

I will be forever grateful for a father who never laid a hand in anger upon his children. Somehow he had the wonderful talent to let them know what was expected of them and to give them encouragement in achieving it. I am persuaded that violent fathers produce violent sons. I am satisfied that such punishment in most instances does more damage than good.

Children don't need beating. They need love and encouragement (Gordon B. Hinckley).[4]

Righteous parenthood would not be reserved for exalted beings if it were a waste of time or an easy task. It would not be considered a celestial work if it brought only a moderate amount of happiness. It is one of those few endeavors that carries over directly into eternity. As we champion and foster our children through their growth, we learn more about God than we can in any other way. Parenthood is a golden opportunity to engage in his favorite work, to attain to his kind of courage, to partake of his kind of joy, and to become, as he is, an embodiment of love itself (1 John 4:8, 16).

Notes

1. In *Wilford Woodruff's Journal,* ed. Scott G. Kenney, 9 vols. [Midvale, Utah: Signature Books, 1984], 5:487; spelling standardized.
2. Boyd K. Packer, "The Shield of Faith," *Ensign,* May 1995, 8; see also D&C 29:48; 68:25.
3. "Standing in Holy Places," *Ensign,* May 2002, 93.
4. "Save the Children," *Ensign,* November 1994, 53.

Chapter 32

GLIMPSES

IF WE BUT KNEW WHO THEY WERE

The dream seemed but a drama of things I already knew but could hardly imagine. It is was a lesson about little children, but it brought to mind the lesson we learn when older loved ones are no longer able to "be themselves." A stroke or other debilitation deprives them of the normal tools for expressing themselves. They struggle to speak or behave as usual. While they are bound in their uncooperative shell, we must be content to know who they really are by remembering how they were. In this confining world, mortals never actually reach the zenith of their ancient dimension. All we have are clues.

In the case of little children, there are no clues. Their small, miraculous bodies hide a total stranger. Wondering out of those mysterious, candle-like eyes is one with an untold past. Even as the child develops the power of expression, the craving to express deep messages is halting and in need of coaching, much as the stroke victim who is full of thought but has lost the cerebral pathways for speech. When, in a testimony meeting, the parent whispers in the ear of the child and the child repeats verbatim, what we hear is not a mimic but a momentary liberation, the unlocking of an enormous message, the fleeting freedom of a fettered soul.

The dream began in a hospital delivery room. My wife was having a baby. The doctor complained of the bloody mess, the crankiness of newborns, and the overall foolishness of having babies. But a calm came over my wife and me. The doctor actually threw the baby into a plastic trash can with all the fluids and tissues of birth. I took the newborn girl into my arms and said, "Now, Doctor, this child is fine." I had a sudden admiration for the marvel of creation.

At first this little child seemed as unknowing as any baby, but after she was nestled in my arms she began to speak to both her mother and me about her surroundings, her name, her gratitude that we had not kept her from coming on her "mission," her fears about coming, and how "silly" those fears had been. She was exuberant and entirely self-assured. It seemed to me that the personalities of premortal people must be healthier and happier than mortal personalities.

Another impression was the attribute of sheer intelligence in premortal people. This child was more intelligent than any mortal. I marveled at the quickness and complexity in her grasp of all around her. More than once in the dream, my wife and I looked at each other, thinking, "How blessed it is to have this child without a veil over her mind." It even occurred to me that our older son would want to play chess with her but that she would win so easily that he would probably just give up chess altogether.

In the hospital nursery, we passed by other children who were entirely unable to express themselves. No doubt the veil was soon to draw itself across their minds, if it had not already done so. These children were an uncanny contrast to the child I held—a child who was permitted simply to be herself. Yet, despite the apparent unknowingness and inexpressiveness of the other children, their mothers, true to life, watched over them with constant devotion. I realized this was a divine instinct for filling the most crucial mission of all.

The little girl freshly emerged from all the blood and discomfort was an exquisite, eternal woman of unimagined refinement and background. Her sweetness seemed like the presence of our Father. But with crushing disappointment I somehow sensed that the veil would soon eclipse her majestic mind, and she too would be reduced to the awful limitations we consider "normal."

I awoke with a new and greater disappointment: this woman that seemed so real was not to be our child after all. There was no hospital, no new baby. I lay in sorrow for a minute. Then came a time of contemplation. I saw how truly the prophets have counseled us regarding the having of children, and how we should honor them, never treat them unkindly, and never train them in the ways of darkness and contention.

It struck me that our way with children is too stern. We can better influence them to be good and obedient through tenderness and respect—the way of heaven. If we knew who they were, we would be more gentle. But we do not quite know. We must believe.

These nobles left high places to join us in a narrow, dark journey. Courtesy befits them. Let us remind them of their origin, their goodly image, their godly heritage. Let us be optimistic, lively, and kindly, as are all the great ones they left behind. Let us keep perspective, having patience. Let us cheer each of them to accept their "mission" without fear. Let us not be sharp and full of demands. Let us not be offended when they fumble in the dark. Let us never degrade ourselves or them by accusing, demeaning interactions. Let us not offend their heaven. Let us teach them the refined ways of their past. Let us hold them within the blanket of Christ's grace.

SOME THINGS DID SINK IN

I recently attended the sixty-fifth birthday party of a lady whose children had gathered to read letters of tribute to her. One in particular seemed to belong here. It is from a son we will call Shaun. He is not a doctor or lawyer or chief executive, as are many of his siblings. He might be described as the "average" one who had had a hard time getting good grades or excelling on the basketball court.

As he described the impact his mother had on him, I noticed two reactions among his family members: their smiles of affection for him and their huge appreciation for a mother who, through all the busyness of raising ten children, never lost sight of who her children really were.

> Well Mom, now that I am a parent I start to appreciate the way I was raised. I'll have to admit that a few things didn't sink in very well. You used to say that I would never lie down on top of a bedspread when I got older. But I do.
>
> I still always squeeze out too much ketchup or mustard on my plate even though I am paying for it. You may not believe it, but I put my feet up on the living room table, and I even eat in other places around the house besides the kitchen.
>
> Funny though, I caught myself telling little Shaun Jr. to take his socks off when running outside. A friend visiting the house looked at me and said it was cold out and he should leave them on. But I remember hearing you say that new socks are a major expense in a large family.

Little Shaun also has this urge to play in the butter. I don't know were that comes from.

When I'm up late with a screaming newborn or sick child, that is just one time I feel indebted for what you did for me. But I am most grateful for all the times you told me I could do anything. You told me again and again not to believe the negative opinions of some of my teachers and coaches.

I realize now that those "special" classes I had were just resource classes to help a struggling student make it through school. I always thought I got to have extra teachers because I was special. Thanks to you, I didn't realize I was a borderline kid.

You don't know this, but in college I worked almost full time so I could hire tutors to help me with most of my classes. I never looked at about a fourth of the test scores I got back. I would study so long and hard, but my scores would often discourage me to the point that I thought about dropping out. I still don't know how I made it through the university or did well in business school. Now that I'm out of school, life is easy by comparison.

In fact, a lot of things now come easy because your soft voice always encouraged me to just keep going. The voice of my mother still speaks to me. Some things did sink in—so well that they changed me forever.

The things I have accomplished in my life I can directly relate back to you and to every time you told me to ignore the grade or the label given me.

You made me what I am. You should write a book some day

titled "How to Build Your Kids' Confidence to the Point That They Don't Even Know How to Give Up."

Your eternally thankful son, Shaun.

HER NAME IS SACRED

The whole world could be filled with books just paying tribute to mothers. But I include this one from a twenty-nine-year-old son who stayed up the night before Mother's Day thinking and writing about his mother. The following is what he read to her the next day:

> It seems that when my faith is most strong, when my spirit is more sensitive, and when my prayers are more penetrating, I always voice my gratitude for my dear sweet mother. Her life will be revered for generations to come. She has truly worn out her life for the sake of her children.
>
> Growing up, I never realized that mothers were supposed to have personal interests or do anything for themselves. It didn't dawn on me that they might want time to themselves or get a break from the endless requests from their children. I somehow thought my mother was immune to all these needs.
>
> Only mothers understand what is meant by "24/7." A constant vigil over a child with a world of needs can wear out even the most capable and devoted. So what does it mean to have many children, all of them supposing that she is there to attend to every whim?
>
> Everyone knows you don't ask your mother, you tell her.

How many nights of sleep have been lost to crying babies or unthinking teens, not to mention the emotional stress that takes away the capacity to rest? How often was she in the emotional "red zone," thinking, "I can't take it anymore"?

And was all this done in the midst of grateful smiles and inspiring praise? Hardly. Can there be any work greater, any load heavier, than that of a mother?

I stand in awe of the woman who brought me into this world, and brought this world to me, all at the cost of putting herself on the altar. Her sacrifice, though I don't comprehend it, is sacred to me. She is sacred. Her sweet name has become sacred.

I call her "Mom," the name God has given her anew with each new child he entrusts to her arms. She earned this name. It is the name I have called out in selfish moments and selfish ways. It bespeaks travail, love, and glory. It bespeaks all that she is and does. It bespeaks all that I am and all that I ever will do. The span of that short name cannot be measured. It shall reach across generations, across the eternities. Its sweet sound will always echo in the chambers of my heart. It bends the knees. It hushes the halls of heaven.

When I bow before my Maker, humbled by his goodness, when I consider his mercy toward this foolish and feeble son, and as I render all the thanks and praise which my whole soul has power to possess unto that God who has granted unto me my life, for the favors and blessings I receive at his hand, I remember my mother.

FILLED WITH LIGHT

Ye must grow in grace and in the knowledge of the truth (D&C 50:40).

A home without the gentleness of grace and the safety of truth is like a house without light. It is both dismal and dangerous. Our Father desires that our homes have the same grace and truth—the same light—that filled the home where he brought us into existence. Light fills a marriage with warmth, and it fills children with security from on high.

I have commanded you to bring up your children in light and truth (D&C 93:40).

Christ's light shines where he is repeatedly invited. His grace softens the way we interact, and his truth transforms the way we feel and think. Nothing could add more to our satisfaction and happiness, for his light is not just an idea—it is real (Alma 32:35). In Part Five we will consider how Christ's light might fill our homes.

Chapter 33

THE GRACE OF CHRIST

Mine Only Begotten is and shall be the Savior, for he is full of grace and truth (Moses 1:6; John 1:14; 2 Nephi 2:6; D&C 93:11).

On one hand, Christ is invariably obedient to the *truth.* On the other hand, his divine nature is balanced by *grace.* He is pure and yet patient with impure people. He is strong and yet labors for the weak. Full of truth, he is firmly loyal to the Father. Full of grace, he is gentle in searching after the Father's wandering and disloyal children.

The word *grace* is reserved for especially kind people or especially beautiful actions. To be graceful is to flow freely. It is to be polite as well as generous. We invite Christ into our homes by being gracious toward family members who are not yet interested in being true. The gospel is essentially a covenant of mercy (Deuteronomy 7:12; Psalm 25:10; Isaiah 54:10; Luke 1:72; D&C 54:6; 64:9–10).

Watching for sin, by contrast, is a morbid and unworthy pastime. It takes no special merit or talent to see flaws and faults. Real greatness forgives. It is pure nonsense to get satisfaction from the mental habits of Satan, the great accuser (Revelation 12:10). The more skilled we are at this kind of thing, the more we resemble him. Why become good at an evil trade?

Ye ought to say in your hearts—let God judge between me and thee (D&C 64:11).

In our harder moments we need a script for avoiding toxic thoughts. We must tell ourselves, "Even in the face of some offense, I will not compare myself with others. If someone must compare me with others, let it be God, who alone knows the territory. It's none of my business." If our thoughts travel this path, our feelings, words, and acts will follow (Mosiah 4:13). Evidently, we can learn to say this in our hearts, for the Lord introduced this script with the words, "Ye ought to" (Mosiah 26:31; 3 Nephi 12:22; D&C 64:9). It is a matter of growth.

Ye cannot bear all things now; ye must grow in grace (D&C 50:40).

Righteousness stands little chance where there is no cheer. Christ is good; goodness is inseparable from love; love is the air of gladness. If we want to be filled with light, we cannot ignore each other's longing for joy.

Grace is larger than justice. Grace must be flexible, courageous, creative, and everlastingly patient. Grace is the reaction of strength. And grace is the best way for weak persons to react to each other. Justice, on the other hand, is neither gracious nor particularly smart. It has the narrow logic of a computer chip. It sticks to its own tiny line of reasoning.

We live with imperfect people, as do those who live with us. Countless things do not help the situation, and some things in particular make matters worse. One of these is the idea that we are stronger or better than other struggling mortals.

What seems to be insidious in the people around us usually turns out to be plain old weakness. One who is disgusted at a person's addiction to tobacco may be helpless in the face of fattening food or mindless television programs. Another who is intolerant of a teenager's craving for social acceptance may be addicted to bitter outbursts of anger. Yet another who has no patience for swearing may be unable to control unworthy thoughts.

Few of us get through life without being whipped now and again by some weakness or another. To say that our weakness at least is not as bad as another's weakness misses the point about the problem of weakness. If I have fewer pernicious weaknesses than another person, I may think that I am closer to the finish line. But the problem is that neither of us has finished, nor can we ever finish until we are helped.

Each weakness calls for a Redeemer to pay for its past damages and to replace it with strength. Two weak people, no matter how they seem to compare to each other, both need attention, forgiveness, and subsidizing from the very same Benefactor. To get trapped in silly comparisons does nothing to invite Christ into our homes. Indeed, comparisons only inhibit the humility we need to win his help. Anyone who needs saving has no business prospecting for guilt in another.

Another thing that aggravates the problem is to demean weak persons with a heated analysis of just how disappointing they are. This removes yet another friend from their universe just when they need a friend. It subtracts from an already waning hope, adding nothing to the determination to change. It heaps up an illusion—a pernicious falsehood—that they are fundamentally unable to ever be good. A careful and angry description of weakness makes it sound awfully permanent. Our reactions do no good if they discourage or embarrass. The murmuring and blaming scripts of contention are the ways of hell (3 Nephi 11:29–30; D&C 10:63).

> *Nothing is so much calculated to lead people to forsake sin as to take them by the hand, and watch over them with tenderness. . . . The opposite*

course has a tendency to harrow up all the harsh feelings and depress the human mind (Joseph Smith).[1]

The gospel offers us a wondrous way to add our part to Christ's great atonement, his holy *kafar,* or cover. It is charity. We have neither his authority to condemn nor his power to redeem. But we have been authorized to exercise his love (1 Peter 4:8).

Even if our charity does not redeem and save, it at least testifies of the One who can. If it does not entirely cure, it certainly invites the Physician. If it does not eradicate sin, it can keep sin from destroying a friendship. If it does not win the battle against evil, it can shield us until the battle is won. Our charity supports repentance.

Of course, certain moments call for a kindly one-liner. But frequent corrections cause more problems than they fix. Friendship is mostly about *not* revising the other. We can go thousands of miles without reacting to other drivers on the road, and we can go even longer—perhaps forever—without leaning on the horn of criticism on the road to eternal life. (It is especially silly to honk at the people in the car with us!) Driving is about sharing the road.

In eternity, it will turn out that all people are precious, well-known siblings. Finger-pointing lacerates their hearts; withdrawing our warmth only chills and stiffens their spirits. Whether they were saints or scoundrels in this life, they will once again be our friends. In light of the long future, why not associate as respectfully as possible in the present?

Friendly feelings are not only a joy but also a preventive. Consider the prodigal son, whose experience while at home persuaded him that his father had nothing but love for him (Luke 15:11–25). On that history of affection, he dared return home.

Peter, the prophet and president of the Church in his day, once sent this good counsel to wives and husbands who wanted to "love life, and see good days":

> *Be courteous: not rendering evil for evil, or railing for railing: but contrariwise blessing; . . . For he that will love life, and see good days, let him refrain his tongue from evil, . . . let him seek peace (1 Peter 3:9–11).*

Note

1. *Teachings of the Prophet Joseph Smith,* sel. Joseph Fielding Smith (Salt Lake City: Deseret Book, 1976), 240.

Chapter 34

Grace at Home

The covenant family is a small replica of God's kingdom. The words and actions of its members are to be treated with gentleness, for they are . . .

> *willing to bear one another's burdens, that they may be light; yea, and are willing to mourn with those that mourn; yea, and comfort those that stand in need of comfort (Mosiah 18:8–9).*

If we keep that covenant, our loved ones will feel it and comprehend the accompanying light (Alma 32:35). We cannot convince our families that they comprehend light when they do not. We cannot assume that they feel peace, comfort, and grace if those qualities are absent from our homes.

A home can accommodate the full range of human burdens. The covenant asks that we share them, whatever they happen to be. By bearing each other's burdens, we bear one another.

Likewise, there is more than one kind of mourning. Mourning is harder to bear than most burdens and harder to comprehend. It may be traced to a breakdown in the central nervous system, a life trauma barely remembered, or personal sin. Perhaps we are unable to trace it at all. It is not required—and may not even be possible—that we explain or analyze or grasp the mourning of others. Their pain is real, and it is not going away on its own. That is enough to bring us to their side.

Can we share another person's cross? Can we afford the time? Do we have the strength? Apparently so, for it is our covenant. And the great secret is that this is the path of joy (Matthew 10:39).

> *Let your labors be mostly confined to those around you, in the circle of your own acquaintance (Joseph Smith).*[1]

We do not, as Christ did, bear every burden. He shows us how to be gracious, and then he puts into our hands—our little sphere of influence—a limited number of opportunities. First among these are the ones at home, beginning with our spouse (1 Corinthians 7:3; 1 Timothy 5:8; D&C 42:22).

> *I say unto you, you shall receive grace for grace (D&C 93:20; see also vv. 12–13, 18–19).*

We receive grace from Christ in return for giving grace to others. To invite him into our home, we need to exercise some mercy of our own. We can cast aside that foul tally sheet on which we once kept track of the mistakes of our loved ones (Matthew 6:12). Since we are "required to forgive all men," we can start with those nearest to us (D&C 64:10).

Because the marriage covenant takes each couple into such unique and private territory, we do not compare one marriage to another. But we must keep doing all we can to strengthen our romance and our particular circumstances. This too is grace, a gift of the heart.

Graceful parents, like graceful marriage partners, do what they can. They keep first things first. They do not let frustration seep in and spoil everything. The more fragile the relationship, the more it needs a positive and unruffled cheer.

> *You can't force your boys, nor your girls into heaven. You may force them to hell, by using harsh means in the effort to make them good. . . . The man that will be angry at his boy, and try to correct him while he is in anger, is in the greatest fault; he is more to be pitied and more to be*

condemned than the child who has done wrong. You can only correct your children by love (Joseph F. Smith).[2]

If our children have hurt us, there is but one thing to do in the gospel covenant: forgive them repeatedly and so entirely that the relationship can again—and again—have a fresh start (Matthew 18:21–22; D&C 64:9; 98:39–40). If our parents have hurt us, it is the same. Certain kinds of hurting may require walls of protection, but we can still live the celestial standard. In the grace of Christ, the child, no matter how old, never stops hunting for some way to bring light into a parent's eye (Matthew 15:1–6).

The grace of Christ begins with his atonement. It then distills upon an individual and spreads to the family, and from the family to a lineage of families until all our human kin have been blessed. The gracious blessings of the covenant flow through the homes of grace that are set up by our covenants (2 Nephi 9:53).

A man or woman who has embraced . . . the principles of this Church, ought to live like an angel. They ought never to be angry with each other (Brigham Young).[3]

The angels this world needs most are the mortal kind, married to each other, living together in grace. The hosts of heaven would then be mirrored by a host of earthly families, each a little mercy squad, pointing their influence first inward and then outward.

And if we do not yet live together in grace, then what? We do just what the Savior's grace summons us to do. We ask forgiveness and try again.

Notes

1. *Teachings of the Prophet Joseph Smith,* sel. Joseph Fielding Smith (Salt Lake City: Deseret Book, 1976), 229.
2. *Gospel Doctrine* (Salt Lake City: Deseret Book, 1986), 317.
3. In *Journal of Discourses,* 26 vols. (London: Latter-day Saints' Book Depot, 1854–86), 1:245.

Chapter 35

THE MADNESS OF ANGER

The way of love and faith is the only happy way through this life. In fact, it is the only way through at all. Unfortunately, many families take another path—the dead end of discord and discontent. As charity covers sins, anger suffocates righteousness (1 Peter 4:8).

Life offers us a constant choice between the heaving surges of anger and the peaceful streamlets of grace. If we do not choose the grace of Christ, we choose the disgrace of Satan. To choose the way of our enemy is madness.

The Lord says, "Be of good cheer" (John 16:33; D&C 61:36). Satan says be downcast, be offended at this and that, be discouraged and discouraging, be negative, cranky, harsh, skeptical, angry, mad.

> *[Zion] shall be the only people that shall not be at war one with another (D&C 45:69).*

This stunning prophecy does more than reassure us that Zion will not be at war. It tells us that Zion's people will not be fighting "one with another." Among the Lord's covenant people, there will not be contention even on a private or family basis. That will be unusual for this old battle-worn planet. It will be a modern miracle: no ill will, no strife, no yelling, no hostility between acquaintances. They will be the "only people" on earth not cursed with the madness of anger.

The miracle must begin in the way we react to anger. It is in that moment when only one person is angry (so far) that anger either loses force or catapults into a miserable cycle. Though we may feel the lash of anger upon our own hearts, we must decide not to spread the pain any further. There cannot be a peaceful latter-day Zion if we get angry at anger (JST, Ephesians 4:26).

Our first mistake is to believe that resentment is healthy, that blame must be assigned, or that we have some right to vengeance. Somehow, these fatal germs of the fallen world can breed in the mind if we believe the wrong things. But the truth is that we have a right—an assigned and wonderful role—to close gaps, show hope, and soften hearts. This does not mean that we should be soft-headed, gullible, or foolish. We are to be redemptive and wise—bigger than anger and contention.

> *This is not my doctrine, to stir up the hearts of men with anger, one against another; but this is my doctrine, that such things should be done away (3 Nephi 11:30; Ephesians 6:4).*

How much conflict should there be at home? A moderate amount? A little? These answers miss altogether what the great Lord of our lives commands us. "Such things"—anger, contention, or anything similar—"should be done away." The commandment sounds as if it means now, within in the hour, today, before the sun sets.

Repeatedly reviewing and rehearsing the same painful events and the same hurts brings to mind the image of a cow rechewing and redigesting its cud. If we do not have the stomach for that image, how can we stomach something even more ghastly: the overripe and bitter refuse of old conflicts, chewed over and over?

Perhaps we believe our disputes ought to be reviewed one more time and that we have a right to all our claims and blames. Wherever we got that idea, it was not from the covenant of peace.

We are not even to rail (which means to speak with contempt or spite) against our worst enemy, Satan (D&C 50:33). Surely it makes no sense, then, to insult or upbraid our loved ones.

If I go all day without taking offense—without bitterness or even complaint—no blessing will be lost. If I should happen to miss something, if I fail to detect blame in some person, so what? Perhaps I can keep this up all year. If I get that far, why not continue in this good pattern for all eternity?

For behold, at that day shall he rage in the hearts of the children of men (2 Nephi 28:20).

The sound of anger is Satan's echo among us. It radiates his presence. To be mad is to be a prosthesis, an artificial limb, for one or more evil spirits. If we cannot detect the darkness of our anger—if we do not notice the vast reduction in light—heaven certainly does.

Some people who live together have developed a tendency, maybe even an addiction, to be easily offended at each other. As a result, their eruptions become commonplace, occurring weekly or even daily. Life at home was never intended to be that way, and it does not need to be that way, even when living with the weak or wayward. We can hardly imagine how the curt and unkindly home strikes observers in heaven, where harmony is an unbroken way of life.

Even the angels, who have the moral authority of heaven, refrain from speaking evil of people. They avoid disdainful words and disrespectful tones about other people's failings (2 Peter 2:9–11). Someday we will have their higher perch, their clearer view, their fulness of light. At that day we will be very glad if we do not have to think back on mortal lives stained with the madness of anger.

Chapter 36

ETERNAL LIFE AND PRIVATE LIFE

Eternal life is the name of the kind of life which God our Eternal Father lives. . . . If we gain eternal life it will be because we advance and progress and become like him (Bruce R. McConkie).[1]

To know our Father, we need to live his way—imitate his goodness, exercise his power, and try his kind of relationships. In other words, we taste his eternal life by experience.

Let us go up to the mountain of the Lord, to the house of the God of Jacob; and he will teach us of his ways, and we will walk in his paths (Isaiah 2:3).

His "ways" and "paths" are family ways and paths. They are presented in a "house," of course.

Heavenly Father and Jesus Christ are actually giving away the secrets of the universe . . . in holy temples and in holy scriptures (Neal A. Maxwell).[2]

The covenant couple relies heavily on the temple. It is the bridge upon which they may escort their family into the eternal world. For example, a timeless standard of modesty in dress, absorbed from the eternal home, is taught there. That standard is then taken into the covenant couple's earthly home. The children sent to that home from constellations above are met with an everyday culture that befits their heaven.

God's ways bid the covenant family to refine their lives on many fronts: manner of speech, treatment of others, choice of friends, selection of entertainment, use of money and time. By living according to the culture of heaven, we create a *worthy* home. If we are to have continuous light, we must face the matter of worthiness.

> *Where two or three are gathered together in my name, there am I in the midst of them (Matthew 18:20; D&C 6:32).*

A lone person can live the culture of heaven in certain ways, but the gospel covenant really unfolds in the warm confines of marriage. Two souls explore the fulness when they become three and then four and so on. The privacy of their tiny gathering is the most promising place for the Father to plant his ways.

Private life—the life of home—is real life, the life that counts. Public life is a supporting atmosphere around the private. If the man seems to dominate the public layer, that is only for custodial reasons. At the center, in the private life of joys and priorities, he and his wife work as equals.

The outer layer gets its worth by blessing the inner layer. We should not be so impressed with the support system that we forget to go home to enjoy its end purpose. Someday, in a more sane and realistic place, the public layer around the family will shrink to its proper, modest proportion. We will be happier then.

Every family has its chosen culture—chosen by the beliefs and desires of its members. Belief and desire create habits, and habits expand, harden, and fill our time with patterns. We speak this way rather than that, we give up this but not that, we are interested in this instead of that. A family chooses more than a culture. It chooses its *mission*—its focus, its hope, its grand purpose.

A family may learn to care a great deal about its favorite TV programs. Some families, without thinking much about it, have adopted that mission. Another family may plan more than anything else for time at the cabin in the mountains. Yet another gravitates around fishing or eating. There are so many things to love and live for, so many combinations.

The mission, whatever it is, will keep everyone busy, eventually consuming our time together on earth. Well-chosen or not, the mission dominates and radiates. Even the entire house of Israel has at times made a collective, communal choice. This family of families has sometimes done the will of the Father but often has chosen to play at lesser things instead.

The private mission of a covenant family can be diluted by settling for less and experimenting with non-covenant ways. For example, when a member of a covenant family marries outside the covenant, a new home is created but with a weaker culture, a mission based only partly upon the eternal plan. This trend offers less and less room for the Father's way of life, until private life and eternal life have little in common.

A small community of our ancient grandparents was once called to protect the place of the covenant in their lives by building a great wall around the temple. When temptation came calling, they knew better than to stop their work. They would not "come down," even for a little break, to discuss other opportunities. One of them, perhaps a great-grandfather to you and me, said:

I am doing a great work, so that I cannot come down: why should the work cease, whilst I leave it, and come down to you? (Nehemiah 6:3).

We sometimes need an iron will to refuse the insistent lures of the world. Our "great work" is to shore up the walls that keep our homes private and undiluted and our families eternal. We cannot afford to come down.

Notes

1. In Conference Reports of The Church of Jesus Christ of Latter-day Saints (Salt Lake City: The Church of Jesus Christ of Latter-day Saints, April 1970), 26; see also Mark 10:30; 3 Nephi 15:9; D&C 88:4; 138:51.
2. In *The Neal A. Maxwell Quote Book,* ed. Cory H. Maxwell (Salt Lake City: Bookcraft, 1997), 222.

Chapter 37

Parents Who Teach

Having been born of goodly parents, therefore I was taught somewhat in all the learning of my father (1 Nephi 1:1).

From the most frequently read verse in the Book of Mormon, we know that good parents teach. Nephi's mastery of practical knowledge is breathtaking (1 Nephi 18:1, 4; 2 Nephi 5:11–17). His parents could not teach him everything they knew, nor did they need to. They taught him "somewhat" in their learning, the summary, the bottom line, the crucial principles that give mastery, the special parts of truth that do the most good. Along with giving Nephi all the other categories of useful knowledge, they made sure their willing, absorbent student had the crucial and guaranteed truths—the Truth itself. Lehi and Sariah followed the pattern originally revealed to Adam and Eve.

I give unto you a commandment, to teach these things freely unto your children (Moses 6:58).

The pattern of parents who teach may be traced back to our heavenly home. An important part of the pattern is to "teach these things *freely*"—without restraint or impatience, with delight and clarity and frequency. "Glad tidings" should be shared gladly, especially when being shared with a glum generation (D&C 62:5). Let the spokesman be cheerful in declaring good news.

Just what shall we teach? The Lord actually gave a little curriculum outline to Adam and Eve. He listed what "these things" are that parents should so freely teach. The list revolves around the role of Christ and the privilege of being stirred by the Holy Ghost (Moses 6:57–63).

The Lord's doctrines are understandable to children, especially if their own parents teach those doctrines with care and patience. But parents must first search the scriptures to get their own grasp of things (1 Peter 1:10; Alma 17:2–3; Moroni 7:19). How hard is that? Surely the Lord would not give this law if those who are able to bear children were not able to teach children. If we allot the time these things deserve, the necessary methods and ideas will distill upon us. But not even the prophets could fill this quest by confining themselves to generalities and putting in a few moments now and then.

> *It were not possible that our father, Lehi, could have remembered all these things, to have taught them to his children, except it were for the help of these plates. . . . Were it not for these things, . . . even our fathers would have dwindled in unbelief (Mosiah 1:4–5).*

If Lehi and the other noble ancestors of King Benjamin would have dwindled in unbelief without the scriptures, that settles the question for us. The clock is ticking, for we must bequeath scriptural truth to our children before their own adult lives unfold. No wonder this parental privilege of teaching is a timeless "law unto the inhabitants of Zion" (D&C 68:26; 68:25, 27–32; Moses 5:12). What Zion could there be or how long could Zion survive without the flow of sacred, saving knowledge from one generation to the next?

> *Thou shalt teach them diligently unto thy children, and shalt talk of*

them when thou sittest in thine house, and when thou walkest by the way, and when thou liest down, and when thou risest up (Deuteronomy 6:7).

The words are best taught if they are first in a parent's heart. Then it will become natural to discuss those words by the glow of dawn, the rhythm of day, or the lamp of evening. It is difficult to see how this blessing could be so gracefully imparted by anyone outside the home, no matter how learned or well-meaning. Eternity seeps deep into the child who repeatedly tastes it in family conversation. Blessed are those children whose parents freely share light with them.

The best time to teach is early, while children are still immune to the temptations of their mortal enemy, and long before the words of truth may be harder for them to hear in the noise of their personal struggles (Henry B. Eyring).[1]

God takes his messengers seriously as they take him seriously (Romans 10:14–17; D&C 138:30). Such messengers love their message and know it is sure (Alma 5:45–47). They deliver it with interest.

If we have successfully sought our God, we are natural guides on the path (1 Nephi 15:14; Abraham 2:12). It is our privilege and pleasure to inspire our children to seek the knowable and personal God of heaven. To skirt this role is to court sorrow. We are reminded of the children of King Benjamin's people who managed to grow up in homes of faith without developing faith of their own.

Because of their unbelief they could not understand the word of God; and their hearts were hardened. . . . And they were a separate people as to their faith, and remained so ever after (Mosiah 26:3–4).

As children, they had not known the Lord. As adults, they were enemies unto him. In that generation, the covenant died among some families for generations yet unborn.

History awaits the care and attention of family teachers. By that effort, on Monday evenings and at other moments through the week, the light of sacred knowledge fills their homes. They are living the eternal pattern of earthly parents and Heavenly Parents who teach.

Note

1. "The Power of Teaching Doctrine," *Ensign,* May 1999, 74; see also D&C 93:40.

Chapter 38

That They May Know of Christ

Most of us mature spiritually by first seeing our duty and later understanding doctrine—from commandment to covenant. Infants digest the simple milk first and the solid stuff later. First come the rules, then the principles (Hebrews 5:12–14; D&C 19:22). It is the job of parents to nourish with more and more substance so that the young may be strong.

> *You might as well try to raise up an athlete on a diet of chocolate bars and soda pop as to attempt to sustain your youth with activity programs only. . . . Sooner or later we will be drawn to do it the Lord's way (Boyd K. Packer).*[1]

Of course, the Lord's way is to bring up our children on "the good word of God" (Jacob 6:7; Moroni 6:4; D&C 98:11). The teaching parent draws from a vast store of nutrients in the standard works and Church magazines.

> *In our family home evenings I hope we will discuss with our children these things and let them taste the sweetness of the truths we have enjoyed. And when the* Ensign *magazine comes out in November, with all of the conference messages, please don't just throw it aside with the comment that you have heard it all, but read and ponder the various messages (Gordon B. Hinckley).*[2]

Right in the center of all our sacred source material—standing in this pillar of light, as it were—is the most nutritious and empowering doctrine of all: the role of Christ in the life of every imperfect person and every unsettling situation. Many upset children, dissatisfied youth, and anxious adults are missing this key of keys or have not yet realized how it relates to their locked lives.

> *We labor diligently . . . to persuade our children . . . to believe in Christ, and to be reconciled to God. . . . We talk of Christ . . . that our children may know to what source they may look for a remission of their sins (2 Nephi 25:23, 26).*

For many, the question really is, "To what source may they look" for the wholeness they once felt as children? Nephi has given us the answer, but for some of our loved ones Christ seems only to be in charge of strict justice and all its rules. Even the religious may forget that he is their family's bosom friend. He is the Lawgiver, and he will be a judge in due time. But his present specialty is to save and redeem.

Unfortunately, no one can be quite so effective as our parent—our very own personal adult to whom we have looked for everything—in distracting us from the encouraging hand of Christ. There is no one quite like a father or mother to create the impression that religion is all about impossible laws and persistent guilt. Even the religious parent can, without realizing it, paint the gospel in this way.

Fortunately, there is nothing like the natural power of parents to help us trust in the gospel's safe harbor so that we see no need to try other shores. To have this influence, parents do not have to be scholars, but they need to feel indebted to Christ, having their own childlike attachment to him. They talk of him at the right times because they think of him at all times. They rejoice in him because of a million mercies, and their appreciation flavors everything. To the child who has weaknesses similar to their own, they are quick to point out the Savior's readiness to help. Their children learn where to look for their blessings.

If they try to create peace by their own effort alone, they will finally have to give up—as so many do—or keep dashing themselves against a task much too big for mortals. They must discover how to come unto him.

> *At that day shall the remnant of our seed . . . come to the knowledge of their Redeemer and the very points of his doctrine, that they may know how to come unto him and be saved (1 Nephi 15:14).*

How is it that we parents and our children may come near to Jesus and receive his help? Here is a review: We do not march right up to him. We do not come unto him by might or intellect or sparkling personality. Nor do we approach him by any other method of our choosing. We approach him in reverence.

We invite his hands to be placed on our heads by "the covenant" itself. The covenant is his. He has laid it out in segments—sequenced and ordered. Each segment is what he calls an ordinance, a covenant-making moment. The ordinances are memorable because they are so simple and yet, being filled with almost endless meaning through symbolism, are so distinct from normal daily experience. We enter after his manner, on his schedule, according to his order.

If we receive the simple ceremonies and make the promises in faith, and if we then remain faithful to them, we will steadily prevail over our problems.

We will discover Christ personally supporting and prompting us to the end. We will soar in our trust of him. His peace will come automatically.

The light will steadily grow brighter until no darkness remains, and "he will unveil his face unto you" (D&C 88:68).

> *Then shall ye know that ye have seen me, that I am, and that I am the true light that is in you, and that you are in me; otherwise ye could not abound (D&C 88:50).*

This gospel feast is not meetings, programs, and awards, for these are the implements—the spoons and bowls—by which we partake of the Savior's banquet. The feast is his assistance and friendship in the covenant (2 Nephi 11:5–6). It is his marvelous, personal light in a life and a household.

Is there a joy greater than this opening of our eyes? If so, perhaps it is to see the eyes of our own children flutter open.

We must not allow our children to misunderstand what is in our hearts. They need to know that they are our treasures and that because of this we share the great plan with them. They should know that we enjoy our calling to teach them of this plan. And they should know that we delight in the Deliverer who has delivered them into our care.

Notes

1. "The Saints Securely Dwell," *Ensign,* January 1973, 89.
2. "An Humble and a Contrite Heart," *Ensign,* November 2000, 88–89.

Chapter 39

Home as a Living Lesson

Homes need the Rock now as never before. Storms on land and sea are but emblems of the bad weather beating on families (Psalm 107:28–30; Isaiah 4:5–6; Mark 4:37–39; Revelation 16:18–21; 3 Nephi 14:25, 27; D&C 115:6).

> *There [shall] be a great forsaking in the midst of the land (Isaiah 6:12; 2 Nephi 16:12).*

While the everlasting covenant spreads from border to border, millions opt for the temporary instead. In an epidemic of quitting, many give up on each other, on themselves, on the plan of God, and on the laws of man and nature—disloyal to the very idea of loyalty. It is the "great forsaking" Isaiah saw. And worst of all, it is at the center, the core, "the midst of the land." In other words, it is in the home itself. It almost seems that there are more real losses than real gains (2 Nephi 27:3).

Satan delights in this scene of undoing and desertion. He hates the family and its Christ. He despises every feature of the covenant. He urges every ruinous idea and insidious doubt that he can. He encourages the idea that our Father's plan is silly or futile, and the harness slips further over precious heads.

The covenant people cannot just sit back and enjoy their blessings. They are witnesses of the greatest storm and workers in the greatest rescue effort in history.

> *Strong opposition will always come against the work and will of the Lord. . . . The work of the adversary will strike directly at . . . the family. . . . Our vigilance cannot be relaxed. . . . We cannot yield to any iniquity without putting our families at risk (Russell M. Nelson).*[1]

After the faithful have been faithful long enough, the mountains of family-threatening trash will be made low, the stylish excuses for sin will be exposed for what they are, and the false wisdom of our time will be set aside (2 Nephi 27:26–27). Our opponent will lose in the end, though he will score a lot of points just before he is thrown out of the game (1 Nephi 22:16–18). Heaven will watch over Israel and then will come right into her midst (3 Nephi 20:22).

Dangers will hover and surround, but in keeping with the promise, they will not endure. Christ's protection will be poured out "according to the covenant" (JS–M 1:20).

In such an hour, can anyone rejoice? Yes! In Zion the joy will be real (Psalm 48:2–3; Isaiah 35:10; D&C 45:67–71; 97:21). Zion's people will carry their bright lamp of hope into earth's dark corners (D&C 45:26–28). Their prophets will declare to mankind—in fact, they are declaring it even now—that "the family is central to the Creator's plan." And they add a solemn caution:

> *We warn that the disintegration of the family will bring upon individuals, communities, and nations the calamities foretold by ancient and modern prophets (First Presidency and Council of the Twelve Apostles).*[2]

So, of all the work we have to do, our work at home is of matchless priority. The home of a covenant person is intended to be a token of the Father's plan, a highlight in the Savior's career, a picture of success for heavenly hosts. It is our most important sermon to a world in disarray.

> *We have no choice . . . but to continue to hold up the ideal of the Latter-day Saint family. . . . We cannot set aside this standard, because so many other things depend upon it (Spencer W. Kimball).*[3]

The Lord tells us that he has restored his way of life to a small core of people, "not for [their] sakes only, but for the sake of the whole world" (D&C 84:48). All mankind needs this living lesson, this clarification of the gospel, this live demonstration of the covenant offered by the Father and Son through you and me. As the Lord's way of life becomes more widespread, the covenant will approach its finest hour.

> *Then will I fulfil the covenant which the Father hath made unto all the people of the house of Israel (3 Nephi 16:5).*

A home filled with light and faith is our best herald of the good news. It serves as an appetizer to the great latter-day banquet, inviting people to flock to *his* house for the rest of the meal.

> *Yea, a supper of the house of the Lord, well prepared, unto which all nations shall be invited (D&C 58:9; 3 Nephi 12:14–16).*

Notes

1. "Set in Order Thy House," *Ensign,* November 2001, 71.
2. "The Family—A Proclamation to the World," *Ensign,* November 1995, 102.
3. *The Teachings of Spencer W. Kimball* (Salt Lake City: Bookcraft, 1982), 294–95.

Chapter 40

GLIMPSES

SMILE

I was the new bishop, and people were still getting used to me in this role. That seemed to come out as one young man stood in testimony meeting and said with kindness and candor, "I'd like to look up to the front each Sunday and see the bishop smiling." I think he was saying that, so far, he had not noticed the new bishop smiling very much.

It happened that the next week took me out of town, and I had time to interview myself over and over. Was I an unhappy or grumpy man? "No, I don't think so." But was I really happy most of the time? "Sure." Well, then, could anyone have guessed? Now and then during the day, I'd check a mirror or a window reflection. "No, not the faintest smile. I'm happy, but it's a well-kept secret."

So, hoping not to be artificial, I tried to smile more. I figured a big showy grin was not the way to go. But how about a down-to-earth expression of good cheer? Could I manage that? It took some remembering. I had to remind my face. But I was out of town. The people around me did not know any better. It was a good time to practice.

After a week of this, I noticed a couple of things. One was that my face gradually did not have to be reminded as often. The positive expression was becoming a little more instinctive. The contentment in my life was showing through more automatically.

Another thing I found was that it was hard to be unkind or angry or to have other selfish feelings on the inside when I was trying to be of good cheer on the outside. I will never forget the moment when that realization hit, though I had heard about the principle all my life.

Furthermore, this new effort was not only affecting me but others as well. A simple little offering, a smile, was making a difference in the world.

What the young man in my ward had prompted me to do was not purely cosmetic after all. This was in some way a spiritual project. Somewhere inside myself the decision to smile was being accompanied by a decision to approach life more happily. To sincerely smile, I had to assume that things were going to be all right in the long run. I had to believe that the people around me might benefit from knowing that another person felt this reassurance. I did not have to say it out loud necessarily. I could cast my vote in favor of life's purpose and simply be pleasant no matter how difficult the passing moment might be.

And if a pleasant expression worked that way most everywhere else, why not at home? Why not at the dinner table, passing each other in a hallway, doing the chores, or discussing the budget? Good cheer seems to do a lot of good when it is not required, when no one demands it, and when the outside world is not watching. We know it from the gracious lives around us and by trying it ourselves: A smile can be a gift of love.

THE PRINCIPLE OF BEING TOGETHER

Now and then we are associated with people who seem to escape our notice for a while, and then one day it dawns on us that they are remarkable.

Certain families are like this. They live the way they ought to, they manage to keep the important things in perspective, they bear the sweet fruit of gospel living, and yet don't call attention to themselves. I asked the mother of such a family about the way she and her husband have tried to raise their children. Her answer was that part of living the gospel together is working and playing together. These are her words:

> When I was growing up I had chores, but I just did them alone. My mother made dinner and worked around the house, but my jobs were separate. Things were different in my husband's family. They had a large garden and his grandparents had a large orchard. They didn't hire laborers for the harvest or at pruning time. Instead, the children and grandchildren became the laborers. The women saw to it that there were meals for all these family workers and that the little children were being watched. They supervised the bottling of fruit and other produce. When I married into this family, it didn't take me long to notice the close and healthy relationships that resulted from all this work together.
>
> Though our family is not perfect, working together and playing together have been a big blessing to us. My husband and I didn't have the benefit of a large orchard in raising our own children, but we have always had a good-sized garden spot. Year after year, the garden never goes away. Our children have been raised with the understanding that everybody helps to cultivate, plant, weed, water, harvest, and put up the produce, just as everybody helps to eat the resulting food for the rest of the year.
>
> The children have always earned their own spending money

and even some of the money for other things like clothes and school expenses. They have done yard work, babysitting, and when we lived in a rural area, they did chores for nearby ranchers.

We have taken on building projects over the years—a garage for us, a house for one of the in-laws, and even a duplex apartment for the grandparents. That was a lot of work, work we did together, and when we go to those places, we remember a lot of experiences together, from hauling forms for the cement foundation to nailing down the roof shingles.

These kinds of things have instilled a certain confidence in our children, a feeling that they can make their way in the world and that they are not afraid of work. They know that work can be rewarding and even fun, especially when we are working together.

But we also have fun when we aren't working! I suppose we have spent more time camping and fishing and playing than most people think possible. We love to go up the canyon to play Frisbee and have a picnic. For the most part, the fun hasn't been very expensive. When our family was small, I recall borrowing a tent from a relative. Soon after that, my husband built a camping shell to put on our little pickup. We took a camping trip from Utah to Mexico one summer using that camper. The Mexico trip was so memorable that we have done it every year since then, at Christmastime. The children have always preferred to have that trip instead of staying home and spending the money on presents.

I remember the old boat we bought and fixed up. There again, we found that you can buy a lot of memories on a small budget. What it does take is time. Time seems to make our love more convincing.

Every family has to decide their ways of being together, but it seems that working together and playing together go hand in hand.

Most of us need to stop now and then and ask, "What can we do to get ourselves back together?" Time together begins not with raising children but in the relationship between husband and wife. Couples, young or old, need time. That, after all, is why they married—to spend time together. And that, after all, is what "eternal marriage" is all about—*lots* of time together! Why not start enjoying eternal marriage now?

ONE FATHER'S PATH TO WISDOM

The following story is about John, a man who is easily honored by those who know him. Many of us know men just like him. His wife explained what has enabled him to do so much good in the world.

John is not slick or smooth in a worldly way. He is a quiet, behind-the-scenes guy who lays the foundation for others. He leads this way in our family and also at work—usually not out in front. He empowers people, especially his own children. He sets things up and lets others get the credit. This isn't a show; it's just his way. If you knew him well, you would sense his depth of wisdom. But you would have to know him as well as I do to know the path he walks in order to lead so well.

Somewhere along the way John figured out that not all

knowledge comes from books. Inspired knowledge comes from whole-souled prayer. And years ago he got into the habit of fasting—short little fasts now and then—when some issue came up in which he felt out of his depth. This wasn't just for major things. It was also for minor things that were saved from becoming major.

For John, it is important to get to bed early and to get up early. He spends that early morning time in gospel study and prayer and in writing down ideas. Some ideas are gospel insights, but many of them are plans—impressions about what to do. He tries to take care of those things as soon as possible.

John may spend one or two hours a day just following up on early morning impressions—making phone calls, writing letters and e-mails, visiting with people or doing some other kind of service to others. Some of it is about family matters, some about Church callings, and some about his work. After doing this for many years, he now has about twelve volumes of thick journals—notes from those morning sessions.

John hasn't become famous or overly impressive to strangers. But many times one of our grown children has called about some worry and said, "Dad, could you inquire of the Lord and write down your impressions? I need some counsel."

Many problems have been solved at work and other places, quarrels settled, marriages stabilized, hearts mended, and souls put at peace because of this one man—a man who always wants to know the Lord's will and then does it.

I have watched over the years as John has gotten the spirit of service and the power of the priesthood right into his soul. To

> him it isn't grueling. He enjoys living close to the heavens and spending his life in service. The joy spills over in our marriage and family.
>
> I believe that my quiet, unassuming husband will one day be embraced by that Being he has come to know so well. His connection with the Lord comes not only in those uninterrupted morning hours while most people sleep but also during the day and evening when he is among people, doing what he knows he should be doing.
>
> I'm sure the Savior with whom he has become so comfortable will someday welcome my sweetheart home. Meanwhile, he quietly carries on. He listens for the still small voice and follows it. His knows it well. I don't think he'll be very surprised when he personally meets the One who whispered to him all those times. I think his lot will be to take his place in the circles of similar men on the other side.
>
> We have raised a large family, so I know something about the price a wife and mother gives to fulfill her calling. But I am so grateful for what my husband does day and night in order to fulfill his. It has made the difference between joy and sorrow for my children and me and for countless other people.

John's path may not be tailored for everyone else. But for each of us there is a personal path that invites wisdom and capacity. When we walk that path, we cannot help but bless people.

Surrounded by Home

In a stunning fusion of reality and symbolism, the Lord spoke through Isaiah:

> *Behold, I have graven thee upon the palms of my hands (Isaiah 49:16).*

The atoning work of Jesus was not confined to the hours he spent on the cross of Calvary, for he entered upon his infinite suffering the night before, in the Garden of Gethsemane. Nevertheless, the wounds in his palms symbolize his whole offering to us. With the hands that will enfold us and join us together, he paid the price that goes with his calling. Having referred to his atonement, the Lord next refers to our homes.

> *Thy walls are continually before me. Thy children shall make haste; thy destroyers and they that made thee waste shall go forth of thee (Isaiah 49:16).*

In Part Six, our purpose is not to be overwhelmed by all the ways we might set our homes in order. We are watching for something here or there that would lift our families and make our Family Friend feel more at home.

Chapter 41

A House of Order

Organize yourselves; prepare every needful thing; and establish a house, even . . . a house of order (D&C 88:119).

This commandment was given for the establishment of a temple, but it applies broadly. God does care about our circumstances, whether in his house or ours. The patterns we follow in our homes, like those we follow in the temple, are ways of inviting the Savior to abide with us.

That wicked one hath power, as yet, over you, and this is the cause of your affliction. . . . If you will be delivered you shall set in order your own house, for there are many things that are not right in your house (D&C 93:42–43).

We long for poise. We want to be in a place where things work smoothly, where life is stable and safe, and where we may be in the arms of love. We want to live after the manner of our Father. We set our houses in order because we long for home.

When we arrive in the celestial kingdom of God, we shall find the most perfect order and harmony (John Taylor).[1]

"Perfect order" is one thing, but harmony is quite another. And yet, they are connected—as much on earth as they are in heaven. To manage our homes by his principles is one more pleasant offering we can make, a sign that we have embraced his way.

Order does not come to pass on its own. Only wisdom and work can counter chaos. The Quorum of the Twelve Apostles has counseled fathers:

> *It takes hard work and planning . . . to build a constant feeling of love and harmony in the home. . . . You must purify and organize your life. . . . You must plan your day as guided by the Spirit of the Lord (The Quorum of the Twelve Apostles).*[2]

We can have more of our Father's unhurried steadiness if we live by his "wisdom and order" (Mosiah 4:27). He always looks ahead. He makes preparations (D&C 38:9; 38:30; 88:74, 119; 132:3). Those who will take time to sit down and prepare will need very little outside advice, especially if they kneel down before sitting down. We can hardly imagine a more serious invitation to Christ than a couple that frequently, prayerfully plans in detail for temporal and spiritual realities.

We cannot know what things are needful until we have decided what we are trying to do. If our family is not sure of its mission, one thing we can be sure of is a lot of wandering and waste. Once we have distinctly adopted the Lord's will as our own, he will support us in getting equipped and establishing our course (D&C 59:20). If we will take care of his things, he will open the way for ours.

In his kingdom, God sets an example of preparation. For example, think of the missionary training centers of the Church, where his servants are carefully trained for their new responsibilities. Or think of the other MTC, the Mormon Tabernacle Choir, whose efforts are never shoddy. After tireless rehearsals, planning, and sacrifice, the Lord adds his blessing.

At home, just as in the classroom, choir, temple, or any other important labor, we work to be useful in divine hands. Even Jesus had to grow in the use of his tools before performing his perfect work (Isaiah 53:2; Luke 2:52; D&C 93:12–14).

To survive in this world takes some management, and this is especially so for spiritual survival. We remember five ladies in a certain parable who ran out of oil because they were not living their spiritual lives with foresight (Matthew 25:1–13).

Consider what it takes to support a covenant-keeping life: praying and pondering the scriptures in private; faithfully and reverently attending our Church meetings; magnifying our callings; preparing our children for mission calls and Church service; teaching the gospel in family home evenings; doing family history and temple work; and being engaged in many other wholesome activities.

We cannot afford to be mixed up about what is important and what is not. We must discern between a humble desire for the needful and a big urge for the petty. Some of us are underequipped for salvation. Some of us are overequipped for recreation. Some are both.

When we have decided what we actually do need in "order" to serve him, determined to do our part of the work, we may present our desires to the Maker and Giver (Ether 3:2; 3 Nephi 18:20–21; D&C 46:30). The blessings we need will come. As they unfold, we put them to use in our mission.

But now and then we may need to remind ourselves that our mission is not about things (Luke 12:15). The good order that leads to harmony ministers to *people,* their hopes and growth, their welfare and worthiness, their fulfillment and relationships. That is why family leaders are always encouraging and communicating, often in personal interviews. They invite family members to set goals, and they help them to reach them. Family leaders make it clear that they will never give up on family members. They give direction but never unkindly. They lead by persuasion and patience. Even when they must be frank, they are not overbearing (Alma 38:12; D&C 121:41–44). They try to lead after the manner of the prophets.

People are the reason, and time is our major resource, for creating order. We navigate our family into eternity by means of time. Freely given time is certainly the easiest gift to understand. Time is the substance with which we prove our love, the medium for showing honor.

Our children accept time as a sincere gift when we play or relax with them. So it is important not to be "busy" and "important" around them. Evidently, spending money is optional, for most of the happy families in earth's history have had none of it. Time is the wealth we should learn to spend with wisdom and courage. We need to trade the petty uses of our time for the important ones, such as joining little children or family members in their chores or finding some form of service or recreation to enjoy together.

When we are in the house, we need to allow ourselves to "be home." Being "available" does not quite count. We need to be *with* our families. We will not lose a blessing by doing so. Generally speaking, the people at home need us more than anyone else does. Warmth and patience and kind conversation and sensing each other's feelings really work, especially when offered at a slow pace.

It is our job to be right in the middle. Our genuine presence, in large and frequent doses, will cast out a legion of sorrows and mistakes. The Lord is delighted when we have the bravery to slow down, the vision to be calm, the spirit to be reassuring, and the time to join in.

Notes

1. "On Priesthood," *Improvement Era,* June 1935, 372.
2. "Father, Consider Your Ways," *Ensign,* June 2002, 12, 14.

Chapter 42

THE LORD WORKETH BY MEANS

The fallen world has never been very friendly to our Father's way of life, but in the latter days, families find it especially hard to keep the covenant. To do the job, especially during such an hour, we need to make good use of tools.

Consider a tool created in another time. The brass plates were prepared to strengthen millions of Lehi's descendants. Young Nephi was just one who helped make that tool available. Many who came after Nephi may not have had his faith to begin with, but the brass plates helped them grow to Nephi's stature (1 Nephi 5:10–14).

The Lord uses people of faith to create tools that then build faith in other people. Here are a few other examples besides the brass plates: the ships built by Noah, the Jaredites, and Nephi; the thousands of lifesaving wagons constructed in Nauvoo by enormous sacrifice and pure faith during the winter of 1845–46; temples and meetinghouses; tithing funds. In addition to these physical objects, the Church itself is a tool, created by mighty faith that in turn nurtures faith. Programs, covenants, and people raised up to have influence, including the Atonement itself, are also sacred tools wrought of hard work and mighty faith in order to spread faith.

> *The Lord God doth work by means to bring about his great and eternal purposes (Alma 37:7).*

When certain tools are combined, the redemptive effect is even greater, such as the Atonement plus a holy book, the Atonement plus an ordinance, an inspired teacher plus an inspired program, or a couple plus a covenant, a house, and a testimony.

The intent is always to elevate. The vehicle or instrument is of worth only if it truly leads us to the living God. If it does not, it is "not of worth unto the children of men" (1 Nephi 6:6). This guideline can help family leaders as they create customized tools to save their families.

We might say that to "administer" is to create such a tool, or, if it has already been created, to put it in reach of others. Administering is setting things in such an order that the system really works. It is a demanding part of blessing people, requiring lonely persistence behind the scenes, wide perspective, and inspired planning. By contrast, to "minister" is to *be* a redemptive instrument. Ministering is actual contact; it is immediate, direct, personal (Alma 35:7; 3 Nephi 7:17; D&C 42:33–34; 107:12; Abraham 1:2; 2:6). Both ministering and administering are godly privileges, labors of love. In the process of setting our houses in order, we do both.

One sacred tool that a covenant couple could produce would be an elevating family record. It would be one way to lead the minds of their children to yet other sacred records. Moreover, it might turn the hearts of their children to their earthly fathers, to the Lord's promises, and to the Lord himself. What better way is there to "persuade men to come unto the God of Abraham" (1 Nephi 6:4) than through a family testament (2 Nephi 25:23)?

> *I shall endeavor to write some of these things upon this record, for the benefit of my posterity that shall come after me (Abraham 1:31).*

Abraham knew that many of us, like himself, would not have immediate fathers to guide us to eternal life. In any case, either to stand in for our fathers or simply to stand next to them, he wrote for the benefit of his posterity. This is just what all couples of the covenant desire to do. The pattern is not only for families on earth but is also part of the order of heaven.

> *For a book of remembrance we have written among us, according to the pattern given by the finger of God (Moses 6:46).*

The earliest generations of mankind, the children and grandchildren of Adam and Eve, were raised on these volumes of story, faith, and revelation. In that age of the world, these were the primers by which the young learned to read and write (Moses 6:5–6). These "remembrance" books were daily *reminders*—sharpening and deepening the otherwise spotty human memory.

But a book of remembrance is only one kind of tool. Other creations, some tangible and some not—whether shared projects, events, gatherings, or traditions—may be fashioned in the home for the salvation of that home and may be created to strengthen an extended family.

Even the children themselves—not only their bodies but also their character and capacities—are perfect "instruments" of faith and glory. The creation story uses the symbolism of clay for good reason. Children come preformed of clay, not of concrete. The clay offers parents some freedom as sculptors, though not for long.

But the greatest creation is not a child. Rather, it is a happy, faithful, and enduring couple. Who creates such a masterpiece? No one person. In addition to what the two individuals themselves contribute to the sum is a lifetime of giving on the part of their parents of the previous generation. These parent couples who preceded and created that new couple have trained and nurtured and polished a child in the ways of the covenant and have then offered that child as a gift to another person in marriage.

Our children—raised to love light and truth, schooled to serve and rejoice in Christ, prepared to enter into our Father's kind of marriage—are our gifts to heaven. But to raise and polish and school and prepare them, we need good tools. If there was a time when parents did not have to rear and prepare their children wisely, if there was once a day when parents did not particularly need to minister and administer in faith, that day is past.

Chapter 43

SPIRITUAL HYGIENE

To have the sweet aroma of peace—the taste of eternal life—in our homes takes some doing. We might call it "spiritual hygiene." Perhaps this special maintenance is the biggest part, yet by no means the only part, of a family mission. Like the physical body, the spirit has to be in good health to face the rigors and threats around it. Stamina depends on regular hygiene. The gospel prescribes nutrients, labors, and even regular rest. We can think of these hygienic things by reviewing the counsel we have received and the covenants we have made.

The most crucial hygiene is daily prayer. To hold in place all else we do, we must stay connected with the great Father. He sent us on our family mission, and it is to him that we hope to return with everyone intact. We must never forget who is both Source and Destination (3 Nephi 18:21; 2 Nephi 32:8–9).

Prayer sets the stage for other essentials of spiritual health. Though the covenant family meets with other families every seventh day to worship, it worships at home every day, instinctively—even hungrily at times—turning to the sacred writings, which were given specifically for nourishing the spirit.

When the seventh day comes around, we renew the covenant status we have before heaven. We live differently on the Sabbath as a sign of where our hearts are (D&C 59:13). On this day of liberation, we are free to savor the honey without the buzz of business or sting of stress. If we have a drab

Sabbath, probably we have missed the point. To the covenant people, the covenant day is a good day (Isaiah 58:13; Jeremiah 17:21; Mark 2:27; Luke 6:9; Mosiah 13:19; D&C 59:10, 13–16). It is a celebration primarily for the home.

It is the sabbath of the Lord in all your dwellings (Leviticus 23:3).

No wonder the promised blessings of Sabbath keeping are so family oriented:

Inasmuch as ye do this, the fulness of the earth is yours, . . . the good things which come of the earth, whether for food or for raiment, or for houses, or for barns, or for orchards, or for gardens, or for vineyards; yea, all things which come of the earth (D&C 59:16–18).

The Sabbath, once it is written in our hearts, creates a place in mortal time to taste eternal life (2 Corinthians 3:2; 2 Nephi 8:7). On those six other days, we retain this taste while also attending to earthly time and earthly things. If we are overly occupied with the temporal, the sweeter flavor dwindles and the powers of the spirit within grow faint. Even a great prophet was affected by overdoses of temporal concern.

At times . . . Brother Joseph . . . found he was spiritually blind and could not translate. He told us that his mind dwelt too much on earthly things. . . . When in this condition he would go out and pray, and when he became sufficiently humble before God, he could then proceed with the translation (David Whitmer).[1]

When the savor of eternal life fades, we begin to lose our fine sense of what is important. Other hungers and interests find their way into the home.

Even our attempts to be good can take on the tint of the world. We drift from the important to the impressive, from the central to the peripheral, from the transforming to the merely busy.

To fight that drift, we attach ourselves to the living prophets. The good taste of our Father's kind of life steadily returns as we get our eyes back on his servants. John the Baptist taught that when we receive the Lord's messengers and their words without reservation, we have a "cloak" for our sins (JST, Matthew 3:34). That is, the protective robe of Christ's righteousness surrounds us and protects us from our own serious mistakes. As we admit the counsel of the prophet into our homes, we permit the Master to join us there also (D&C 52:36).

The trick is that the guidance of prophets may seem *optional.* A dramatic illustration is the story of Haun's Mill. Some have wondered why Joseph did not give more forceful direction to Brother Haun and his people living at the mill. This comment from Joseph's mother reminds us that the Lord's way is to let families freely decide what they will do with the words of the prophets.

> *It may be said that, if Joseph Smith had been a Prophet, he would have foreseen the evil, and provided against it. To this I reply, he did all that was in his power to prevail upon his brethren to move into Far West, before the difficulty commenced, and at a meeting, three weeks previous, he urged the brethren to make all possible haste in moving both their houses and their provisions into the city. But this counsel appeared to them unreasonable and inconsistent, therefore they did not heed it (Lucy Mack Smith).*[2]

Nobody in heaven and only a fool on earth imagines that a family could gain eternal life by human means. And yet the Lord leads us there ever so gently. He will not compel us to keep up (1 Nephi 20:17). His ways are optional, and his presence is delicate. The covenant couple invites the taste of heaven into their home with the same regularity and for the same reasons that they clean and eat and sleep. With everything at stake, they see to the spiritual hygiene of their home.

> *Abraham was guided in all his family affairs by the Lord; . . . was told where to go, and when to stop; and prospered exceedingly in all that he put his hand unto; it was because he and his family obeyed the counsel of the Lord (Joseph Smith).*[3]

Notes

1. In B. H. Roberts, *A Comprehensive History of The Church of Jesus Christ of Latter-day Saints,* 6 vols. (Salt Lake City: The Church of Jesus Christ of Latter-day Saints, 1957), 1:130–31.
2. *History of Joseph Smith by His Mother, Lucy Mack Smith,* ed. Preston Nibley (Salt Lake City: Bookcraft, 1958), 292.
3. *Teachings of the Prophet Joseph Smith,* sel. Joseph Fielding Smith (Salt Lake City: Deseret Book, 1976), 251–52.

Chapter 44

DESTINY BY COUNCIL

Counsel with your family members and encourage them to participate in the important decisions (L. Tom Perry).[1]

When we were still together in the premortal world, decisions were made in council. This kind of leadership is part of the heavenly order. God neither imposed his will nor compelled our will. Of course, this probably meant that some decisions moved slowly. But unity was more important than speed.

When members of an earthly family gather in council, they are practicing on their small plot of rough, earthy terrain what they once experienced in a well-managed paradise. Their wise decisions and sweet unity can be something like heaven, even at the most ordinary kitchen table.

If family leaders find the going slow, they might remember the patience of the Man of Council. If they are tempted to forcibly squelch various opinions in council, they might remember just who it was in those ancient councils that tried to force his ideas on the group (Moses 4:1–4).

> *Too often we use communication periods as occasions to tell, dictate, plead, or threaten. Nowhere in the broadest sense should communication in the family be used to impose, command, or embarrass. . . . In family discussions, differences should not be ignored, but should be weighed and evaluated calmly. One's point or opinion usually is not as important as a*

healthy, continuing relationship. . . . How important it is to have discussion periods ahead of decisions (Marvin J. Ashton).[2]

The Atonement offers to make us once again "at one" with the Father in his presence. Leadership by council is one down-to-earth means by which the at-one-ment gradually comes to pass. Councils can make us at one at home.

When you are united, your power is limitless. You can accomplish anything you wish to accomplish (Gordon B. Hinckley).[3]

Council leadership calls for maturity, for its purpose is not to dominate, dictate, censure, or fix people. It is an opportunity to see eye to eye, to consider mind to mind, and then decide heart to heart. Each person in the council tries to understand what is wise in the matter at hand. All contribute by expressing their views and by listening carefully to the views of others. The leader helps this happen without goading or being overbearing. The leader is the best listener of all.

Various pieces of the puzzle might emerge from anyone in the council. Often, the one we least suspect to have the answer will contribute the piece that brings everyone together. All, including the leader, try to see the truth despite their previous opinions.

No man is capable of judging a matter, in council, unless his own heart is pure; . . . we are frequently so filled with prejudice . . . that we are not capable of passing right decisions (Joseph Smith).[4]

"Having a say" is not the aim of a council. The aim is to let the inspiration we pray for come naturally through respectful discussion. The leader has tremendous influence on whether this happens, encouraging the shy to speak, reminding all to listen, setting an example of humility, and remembering that the direction to be taken may not have even been imagined when the council first began.

It is not right for us, before going into council, to commit ourselves to any line of action, nor to any decision (George Q. Cannon).[5]

We want the Lord to have *his* say. It may be through this person or that person or a blend of both. In proportion to our spiritual maturity, it will not matter to us whose opinion turns out to be right.

Let no man think he is ruler; but let God rule him (D&C 58:20).

Sometimes we are so eager to have a voice that we do not receive voices, including the still small one. And when our turn does come, we should consider whether the thing we were so eager to say is a real addition. Otherwise a meeting can become blurred with repetition or aimless comments. This does not just misuse time but may also quench inspiration and unity.

Without meaning to, we can undermine a council by overloading it with private comments, covering too many things in one meeting, or approaching decisions too casually or too hastily.

The same principles that apply to a family council apply to a couple council. Husband and wife are on equal footing. They meet with open minds, open to each other's viewpoint and inspiration. Unselfishness is the key.

The father and the mother get together. They want to come to some conclusion respecting some enterprise perhaps; it may be respecting a son or a daughter—the course to take in relation to that son, the best advice to give to that daughter. How should they come together? Should it be with their

> *minds fixed; the mother determined that she is going to have her way; the father determined that he is going to have his way, he being the head? No; the father and the mother should come together, . . . not with any preconceived ideas and a pre-determined plan; for when that is the case, then the manifestation of the mind of the Lord is withheld so that we cannot, under such circumstances, receive the light of the Spirit (George Q. Cannon).*[6]

Creation comes from combining and uniting. This is represented everywhere in nature. It is true in the creation of things and of life. It is true in doing and in being. It is true in arriving at a higher feeling, in planning a trip, and in making a decision that will affect lives yet unborn.

We read that Lehi's family was "led with one accord into the land of promise" (1 Nephi 10:13). To be in "accord" means to be lined up, united, in harmony. "Accord" is related to the musical term for blended notes: chord. Lehi's family was supported by the hand of God only when they were in harmony with the Lord and with each other (1 Nephi 16:29; Alma 37:41).

When we read of that family's long, miraculous passage across deserts and oceans to the promised land, we learn about our own family journey. Wise decisions await our councils. Progression awaits those wise decisions. Our destiny awaits our harmony.

Notes

1. "Called of God," *Ensign,* November 2002, 9.
2. "Family Communications," *Ensign,* May 1976, 52.
3. "Your Greatest Challenge, Mother," *Ensign,* November 2000, 97.
4. *History of The Church of Jesus Christ of Latter-day Saints,* ed. B. H. Roberts, 7 vols., 2d ed. rev. (Salt Lake City: The Church of Jesus Christ of Latter-day Saints, 1932–51), 2:25.
5. In *Collected Discourses,* comp. Brian H. Stuy, 5 vols. (Salt Lake City: B. H. S. Publishing, 1987–92), 2:91.
6. Ibid.

Chapter 45

A Covenant of Work

The youth were having a service project for an older couple in our ward. As time for a break approached, one of the mothers came to drop off refreshments. As she paused to watch, I noticed her casual expression turn to uneasiness. Then she looked at me with a sigh of resignation.

"What?" I asked.

"Oh, just as I feared. Not only does my son not work at home, he doesn't work in public either. I'm afraid he doesn't know how to work, same as some of these other kids." She arranged the refreshments on the table and added with a good-natured smirk, "I wonder, what are we *refreshing* here?"

As she left, I looked at the scene and had to agree. Every one of these young people was good and lovable, but a few hesitated to stay with any particular task for more than a few minutes. It was as if they were confused by a bit of boredom or fatigue, unaware that perseverence is not fatal. They did not seem to know about the personal satisfaction of persisting and perspiring until a thing is finished. Perhaps that mother, as she drove away, was asking herself if there was some way she could teach her child how to work. It is a good question for all latter-day parents.

As Mount Zion looms ahead of us and above us, the rising generation will need to finish rising and to cope with those rising slopes. For good reason, God has called the last labors of this "last time" a "marvelous *work*" (1 Nephi 14:7; D&C 18:44).

> *Hard work moves the work of the Lord forward, and if you have learned to work with real integrity it will bless your lives forever. I mean that with all my heart. It will bless your lives forever (Gordon B. Hinckley).*[1]

Forever? Perhaps the greatest product of our work will be the personal attribute we develop for *lasting*—the resolved mind, the godly attribute of giving steady, unrelenting, ungrudging effort. We must not leave this ingredient out of our personal makeup or family life, for it pertains to eternity.

We cannot keep the covenant without work. Consider this principle, a somewhat overlooked way of inviting the Savior into our families:

> *Cease to sleep longer than is needful; retire to thy bed early, that ye may not be weary; arise early, that your bodies and your minds may be invigorated (D&C 88:124).*

The principle comes with a promise: invigoration of body and mind. Half of the principle is to be up and doing before the world's day begins. That sounds noble, but the other half of that law, to "retire to thy bed early," is the part that makes the noble part possible. Those early hours can be powerful, even sacred, but there is a price: subtracting an hour or two from late-night activities. We send the invitation at night, and he joins us in the morning. It is an act of faith . . . and work.

> *I will show thee my faith by my works (JST, James 2:15; 2:18).*

By my faith, God can begin to work through me, but by my work, he can finish.

Work is getting the job done, enduring all the way through. A family that does not work together does not work. It neither finishes its journey nor progresses in its journey. Work starts the job from an uninteresting beginning.

It continues the job through tall hills and dark passages. It finishes the last details, despite the strong temptation to say, "Oh well, that's good enough."

The good things . . . must be paid for in advance (Boyd K. Packer).[2]

The work of faith begins in a mind that can be taught. The work of faith is finished by a mind that is firm. At its core, the ability to work might be what the revelations call "firmness of mind" (Jacob 3:1; 3:2). Mormon points out that angels associate with those "of strong faith and a firm mind" (Moroni 7:30; 7:29). By an unswerving mind, we hold our course through every murky question and mortal storm. We need such minds in order to know heavenly beings and in order to *be* heavenly beings (Matthew 24:13; 1 Nephi 22:31).

Wherever there is a body of people upon the face of the earth that has nothing to do, that quorum or body will die spiritually. The Spirit of God will not be with men who are inactive (Abraham O. Woodruff).[3]

The military triumphs described in the Book of Mormon illustrate the mighty combination of faith and fortitude—mighty work crowned by mighty miracles. The defensive banks of earth around Nephite cities, topped by works of timbers, can only mean that this saving idea required months of arduous work for a whole nation (Alma 48:7–8; 50:1–6). Millions of baskets of hard-packed soil and rock, dug from the perimeter of city after city, had to be hauled from here to there. And that was just the excavation stage.

Inspired solutions are not always easy ones. We should not be surprised if the Lord offers glorious blessings to a family by an invitation to work. It is how covenant people prosper (Ether 10:22–28).

God follows through; he carries out the plan (2 Nephi 24:24). He is not daunted by the steps that must be taken, nor does he hesitate to take on more children and assume more responsibility. Again and again, he willingly enters upon wide and robust cycles of work (Moses 1:39; 7:30).

This is my work and my glory—to bring to pass the immortality and eternal life of man (Moses 1:39).

The harvest comes to pass through diligence and patience (Alma 32:41–43). It is so in earthly seasons as well as in eternal seasons. The taming of the soil softens and grooms the soul. Work supports life on the outside and refines life within. The Creator breathed so much potential into the forces and factors of the temporal world that they need constant intervention. The elements are so tame and useful when attended, so mutinous and treacherous when ignored. It is a law of life.

Even in higher worlds, however luxurious and cooperative the elements may be, they will always need active governance. We will not do our work in pain and weakness there, but we will work nevertheless and in the best sense. We will take initiative and stay on top of things. Even the most celestial influence needs a pulsing, conscious exertion—a big heart, an open eye, a focused mind, an active hand. The basic law of effort in this world is a good preparation.

Two familiar twins stand before us almost daily and demand that we favor one—not both. They are, "Do it now" and "Put it off." Choose the first and you emerge weary, but at peace. Select the second, and frustration is your constant companion (Thomas S. Monson).[4]

Notes

1. "Inspirational Thoughts," *Ensign,* August 2000, 5.
2. *That All May Be Edified* (Salt Lake City: Bookcraft, 1982), 107.
3. In Conference Reports of The Church of Jesus Christ of Latter-day Saints (Salt Lake City: The Church of Jesus Christ of Latter-day Saints, April 1898), 21.
4. In "Master Builders of Eternal Houses," *Church News,* 24 April 1993, 4.

Chapter 46

GETTING THINGS DONE

But be ye doers of the word, and not hearers only, deceiving your own selves (James 1:22).

A covenant-keeping home is a home of gospel action instead of gospel pausing or gospel posing. Gospel indolence—puttering about when there is some good thing to do—suggests a religion discussed and considered but not yet loved, not taken seriously. To a family stuck on "pause," the Lord might say, "See that ye are more diligent and concerned at home." In fact, he did say that once, adding this warning: "Or they shall be removed out of their place" (D&C 93:50). Families of "doers" have the promise that they will keep their eternal places.

"Doing" puts iron in our diet. Everything in the Garden of Eden grew easily, with the exception of Adam and Eve. So they had to leave. To be equal to the ages, a marriage needs to do things and face things (Genesis 3).

I will go and do the things which the Lord hath commanded, . . . he shall prepare a way for them that they may accomplish the thing which he commandeth them (1 Nephi 3:7).

When Nephi said he would do "the things" on the Lord's list, he meant all of them. That list grew and branched into sublists as his family progressed. Think of how many blessings that family generated as long as they continued their work. We invite the Lord in when we welcome into our families his list of things to do.

But there is something else in Nephi's famous statement. The Lord prepares a way to do "the thing"—singular—"which he commandeth." He abides with us all through the list, item upon item, assignment after assignment, but generally we only have to tackle *one* thing at a time. In fact, there is no list, except for the one we create in our minds. We have but one thing at a time "which he commandeth" us to do.

The old motto "Do it now" is not only about doing things "now" but also about knowing first what "it" is. To be busy with many lists and many extraneous things gives our children the wrong impression about the law of work. They should know that we all have only one thing to do at a time.

For the family leader to "do *it* now" means both to do a chore and to choose wisely. Sometimes it takes brave honesty to admit the importance of one chore and the unimportance of another. Chores such as spending time to prepare thoughtful and enjoyable family home evening lessons, making phone calls and writing notes that make a difference, nurturing relationships, and magnifying Church assignments invite Christ into the home. They are, therefore, infused with the companionship of the Spirit.

> *The greatest joys of true married life can be continued. . . . But this will never fall into place of its own accord (Spencer W. Kimball).*[1]

When we neglect our homework, the effects can be tragic, though generally no one is looking over our shoulders as we might look over the shoulders of our children. In fact, there are important things no one else knows we should be doing. We could cover a little child with another blanket on a cold night. We could do something about the spiders in the attic. We could fix that plumbing problem now before it worsens when no one is home.

The child will not get up to find her own blanket; she'll just be cold all night. It is up to an adult—a leader who is responsible for other lives—to get up and cross the cold floors to put another blanket on that child. "But I didn't know" and "I didn't think of it" will not work. The job of a leader is to find out the need, to think of the blanket and the other things that make a difference.

If we want our children to love their work, we must work *with* them. And while we are working, we can be nice about it! We can treat work not as a punishment but as a good part of the day. We have every reason to be friendly while working together. We can remember that our children are not employees or servants. They are partners. We may force them to work, but we cannot force their will or their willingness. Willingness bubbles up from respect. We gain their respect only by earning it and returning it.

And we should remember that we are not work worshippers. Chores were made for man, not man for chores. If we live for chores, life becomes pointless and circular, shaped something like a shackle. If children rise each day merely to clean a dish or pick up a mess or a toy, they could wonder, "Why rise at all?" Forced labor does not create hardworking people.

With the words "It is finished" (John 19:30), Jesus bowed his head at the triumphal close of his sacrifice and accepted the last drop from his gruesome cup. We shudder at those words with boundless gratitude. Jesus later described the job modestly: "I partook and finished my preparations unto the children of men" (D&C 19:19). It is a great thing to do the Father's will, especially to do it so thoroughly that the job is *done.*

Jesus has paved the way for doers. It will be worth all the work when we have finished and when we hear his sincere voice speaking to us: "Well done" (Matthew 25:21, 23).

Note

1. *The Teachings of Spencer W. Kimball,* ed. Edward L. Kimball (Salt Lake City: Bookcraft, 1982), 297.

Chapter 47

THE LAW OF HOME

As the body is a tabernacle to the spirit, so a house is to the family. A body holds the spirit of one; a house holds the spirits of several.

In our world, the spirit of man expresses itself primarily through the physical body. With our physical bodies, for example, we kneel in prayer, we serve others in various ways, we comply with the Word of Wisdom, we speak kind words, and we do countless other things as physical expressions of decisions made in the spirit self. The body, unless it somehow becomes a prison, extends the influence and will of the inner man.

There are other layers of expression beyond the body. Clothing is an immediate layer. Another layer that extends the spirit is the automobile—bigger and stronger than the body but controlled by the spirit of the driver. Tools, words, musical instruments, telephones, computers, and money are also extensions of the core. They offer opportunities for the spirit to make a statement while in the mortal world.

A house is a giant layer of opportunity. Like the physical body, it is a statement of beliefs and preferences. A house becomes a home when it becomes a layer of protection, a place for things that last, a tool by which we maintain strength in the spirit that lives at the center of all those layers. We might call this "the law of home." We cannot ignore the influence of our bodies, and we cannot be independent of them. Nor can we pretend that there is no law of home. Home affects and expresses our very souls.

That wicked one cometh and taketh away light and truth, through disobedience, from the children of men, and because of the tradition of their fathers. But I have commanded you to bring up your children in light and truth (D&C 93:39–40).

In the culture of home we either remember or forget the covenant, we either invite Christ or turn him away. The Spirit of the Lord is drawn to worthiness—the worthy home as well as the worthy soul. The home is a place where blessings are lost or gained, where hearts either fail or prevail. Where there is faith in the truth, there will be light. If this light fills a home, the hearts therein are wrapped in layer after layer of Christ's power.

The law of home offers an absolute "refuge and strength, a very present help in trouble" (Psalm 46:1; 57:1). It works because Christ is so enormous, so real, and so available. As whole families, as partial families, or as individuals, we are inducted into his friendship by the ageless covenant. Our home becomes his. We invite him inside in ways large and small: we attend meetings at his church, accept his servants, live his standards, participate in his programs, receive his ordinances, carry his name more carefully than we carry our own, study his written words, do his work, enjoy his inspirations day by day, embrace the family connections he has granted us, and seek continually for his healing hand to be upon our loved ones.

In this way the home becomes a refuge, a haven of his peace (D&C 45:66; 115:6). This relief comes "because of the anointing" (Isaiah 10:27; 9:4; 2 Nephi 19:4) and the special gospel status we have accepted. It transcends our location on earth and our spot in history.

From the prophecies of scripture and from the daily news, we have some idea of where history is headed in these days. Evidently, illness and financial hardship will persist, nature will continue to be disturbed, and human conflict will increase (Zephaniah 1:15; D&C 88:91).

What of the covenant people living in this troubled time? And what of their homes? When it seems that our spirits must sink with despair, when the winds build up and the family seems vulnerable to the storm, we can stop to consider the promises. We can take solace and energy from our testimony that the covenant is real.

> *Put upon thy servants the testimony of the covenant . . . that thy people may not faint in the day of trouble (D&C 109:38).*

The roots of the word *home* mean to enclose, cover, make safe,[1] reminding us of the *kafar* robe that represents the Savior's atonement. The law of home permits a household to be clasped in the arms of Christ (Mormon 5:11; Alma 34:16; D&C 6:20). By this principle, home conditions should be much better than world conditions.

Note

1. *Noah Webster's First Edition of an American Dictionary of the English Language* (1828; republished in facsimile, San Francisco: Foundation for American Christian Education, 1967), s.v. "home."

Chapter 48

GLIMPSES

STRESS VERSUS COURAGE

Much of the stress we experience in life comes from trying to do too much and accumulate too much. Since we are the source of this type of stress, only we can filter it from our lives. Filtering requires a vision of what is important. The following suggestions are useful only if we have the courage to act on that vision.

- Stress does not usually come from slow traffic, bad news, or hectic schedules. It comes from letting so many unimportant things into your life that you do not have room for the important ones. If you let too many things into your schedule, it is hard to spend time with your sweetheart. The result is that you get a little too businesslike, rushing past each other from one unimportant chore to another. Maybe you even get a little irritated if the one you love keeps you from doing something. That is not good, and it is not courageous.
- Admit what is important and then give it the time it deserves. Admit what is not important and then refuse to lavish precious time on it.
- As with time, so with money. If we spend big on what does not matter, we only have a few pennies left for what matters most. Some people say we should not bother about money because life is not about

money. But that is just the point. We had better face our finances and control them, or else life *will* be about money!

- Even if just one of you earns the money or pays the bills, do these three things with your spouse: plan goals in writing, making sure that one of your goals is to save; establish a monthly budget for reaching your goals; follow your budget.
- If you cannot avoid all debt, at least avoid consumer debt. Consumer debt occurs when the item you buy depreciates faster than the rate at which your are paying it off.
- Clutter is not just about things; it is also about space. Like time and money, we have a certain amount of space to spend, and we want to spend it on what is important. Our frame of mind will be better if our homes and yards and garages and offices are clean and well-kept.
- Sometimes people fill up their spaces with stuff and forget the most important "things" that go there: people. If there is barely enough room for our possessions in a particular room but not really enough room for us, we have left out the crucial furniture. Making room for people can be a sacrifice, but it is worth it.
- Too many noises can be as hard on us as too many things.
- When an item comes up that needs our attention, deal with it right away. Store it or answer it or pay it or wash it or file it or fix it or throw it away as soon as you can. To set it down or stuff it somewhere means that you have to relive the moment again.
- Get rid of things you do not need. If you do not use it, or if it is broken and you are not going to fix it right away, or if you really do not have room for it, remove it from your life. One of our worst enemies is anything that impedes our lives.

- If something is valuable but not to you, give or sell it to someone else. In the business world, storing things properly is a time-consuming and expensive job. It is not right for us and our loved ones to be stuck in that business when there are so many better things to do in life. It is better to spend space and time and money and emotional strength saving people rather than things.
- A house or room full of jumbled items can be like a prison. Your possessions are like prison guards holding you captive, and the convenient places you need for keeping your few useful and meaningful objects are all used up with "rubble."
- You ought to be able to look around and see reminders of your purpose in life.
- "What should I get rid of?" is not usually the best question. Instead, ask, "What do I need to keep?" Whatever is not really needed is probably really unneeded.
- Few facts, papers, and objects that come to you in this world are worthy of your time or space. Fear clings; faith lets go. Remember how hard it is to open a door when your hands are full? You are in this world primarily to open doors.
- Remember the handcart pioneers. Some of them took so much with them that they could not quite finish the journey.
- Set your house in order, not just your things. It does little good merely to rearrange stuff or repack it in new ways. That organizes the stress but does not remove it. To set a house in order is to make it available. Try to match your home with your purpose in life. That is what the Lord's house does. Everything there matches its purpose.

- The beauty and spirit of the Lord's house depend somewhat on the simplicity and open space we find there.
- A certain amount of rubble may be necessary in life, but do not let it take over.
- If we are going to have things, they should at least make us more, not less, effective. And they should make us more available and lovable.

These little efforts to put a house in order work only if they invite the Spirit of the Lord into a home. Stress is not there when his Spirit is there (Alma 60:23; D&C 45:32; 87:8; 101:22, 64).

LIKE A VIEW FROM THE SPIRIT WORLD

A couple recently told the following story after returning from a twelve-month mission. Because they traveled frequently and stayed in small hotels or homes, they had limited themselves to a week's supply of clothes and few personal items.

"After visiting with the stake president and bishop and some family and friends, and wandering around in our empty house, we drove down to the storage facility where our belongings had been all this time," the wife explained. "We planned to get a few casual clothes and start planning the move back into our home. The facility was full, from floor to ceiling."

The husband said, "I started looking for a couple of shirts in some of the boxes while my wife opened another box in search of shoes. The boxes were full of things we had completely forgotten, things we hadn't cared about or needed for twelve months. I wondered why I should start up again caring about them. Box after box like that."

His wife smiled and said, "We just looked at each other and laughed, feeling so silly. It was like we had died and were looking back from the spirit world and could see how silly all this stuff was. But we weren't in the spirit world and we had a decision to make. We each knew what the other was thinking.

"My husband finally asked, 'Well, what do you want to do?' I told him, 'Let's go back to the bishop's house.' He said that was what he hoped I would say. So we went and put in our papers for another mission!"

That is not a story about people who are too lazy to haul things back to their home. It is a reminder of what little we need and of all the unnecessary things we add to what we need. It is not a story about the advantages of living out of a suitcase, but it does say something about the joy of serving and about the good sense of living so that we can be useful to the Lord.

Does this possession or that pastime contribute to our mission on earth? That is a good question for every family to answer. The best time to face that question is right away, while the answer can do the most good.

Sealed to Heaven

Fortunately, many people on earth honor Christ as the One who saves. But unfortunately, most of those people are not sure what it means to be saved or how to go about inviting him to save them. Most would be surprised to find out that his salvation pertains to families.

I will contend with him that contendeth with thee, and I will save thy children (Isaiah 49:25; see also 1 Nephi 21:25).

His greatest gifts are family gifts. His sweetest healings are family healings. His highest promise is the promise to save us in families.

I have thought many a time that if I labored until I was as old as Methuselah and by that means could have my family dwell with me in glory in the eternal worlds, it would pay me for all the pain and suffering I could endure in this world (Wilford Woodruff).[1]

We invite the Savior into our homes by the covenant. He accepts our invitation. But if some of those we love the most do not accept him, then what? What does it mean to be bound to him and to each other? What are his promises?

Chapter 49

THE RIGHTEOUS NEED NOT FEAR

In their fierce love, parents will do anything to protect their children from the threats and sorrows of the world. But there is a kind of cold from which physical clothing cannot shield our children. There are certain hungers untouched by physical food. There is a truth that secular education will not reveal. There is a dreariness that the most festive surroundings cannot remove. If parents do not accept these realities, perhaps their children will have every good thing except peace.

In the midst of plenty, the peace of Christ can be missing. In the midst of hardship, this peace can be full. It can skip past the unimportant puzzles and bathe the mind in light. Without bothering to sort out boiling human conflicts, his peace will remove hostilities, cancel self-seeking agendas, and inspire fellowship.

The serene assurance that we and our children crave is the exclusive, personal property of the Prince of Peace. When it comes to us, it comes directly from his pure heart, his settled and all-knowing mind, and his quiet and actual presence. He paid the price of that assurance. He worked things out with the strict universe. Now, on his simple terms, his peace can proceed directly from him to our home (John 14:27).

Everyone needs his peace. The best of us do, and the rest of us do, whether prosperous or poor, educated or ignorant, well or ill. Whether our children are pillars in the community or outlaws, whether they are easily pleased or depressed, they need that peace "which passeth all understanding" (Philippians 4:7).

I would speak unto you that are of the church, that are the peaceable followers of Christ. . . . I judge these things of you because of your peaceable walk with the children of men (Moroni 7:3–4).

So spoke the prophet Mormon in the last hours of Nephite history as he met with a gathering of covenant people. He called them "the peaceable followers of Christ" because that gift from Jesus was so evident in their "peaceable walk" among others. How could they be kind and unruffled amid violence? They had the blessing that in the Hebrew is called *shalom*—the utter safety and wholeness that cannot be touched by outward ills. Their rapport with Almighty God was secure, their sins were forgiven, their former sinful tendencies healed.

Because they were true to the covenant, the Prince of Peace was among them. Had we been in that assembly, we too would have enjoyed his presence. Had we gone to their homes—whether commodious city houses or simple shelters in the wild—we would have sensed it. Had we visited their families—whether whole or stricken by death or divorce—we would have felt that they were sealed to heaven.

He has set heavenly beings to watch over us and to guard us from the attacks of evil powers while we live on earth. Do we realize that in our daily walk and work we are not alone, but that angels attend us wherever our duty causes us to go? (James E. Talmage).[2]

The friends of Christ on earth attract powerful friends of Christ in heaven. Therefore, there is no reason for the usual discouragements to discourage them or for the usual terrors to terrify them (Romans 8:31).

> *I took occasion to gently reprove all present for letting [the] report excite them, and advised them not to suffer themselves to be wrought upon by any report, but to maintain an even, undaunted mind (Joseph Smith).*[3]

> *If God be for us, who can be against us? (Romans 8:31).*

The covenant home does not have to live with the distress so common in the world because the covenant home qualifies for countless promises, including:

- *My kindness shall not depart from thee, neither shall the covenant of my peace be removed (3 Nephi 22:10).*

- *Keep all the commandments and covenants by which ye are bound; and I will cause the heavens to shake for your good, and Satan shall tremble and Zion shall rejoice (D&C 35:24; 21:6).*

- *He will preserve the righteous by his power. . . . Wherefore, the righteous need not fear (1 Nephi 22:17; 22:22).*

- *For God hath not given us the spirit of fear; but of power, and of love, and of a sound mind (2 Timothy 1:7).*

- *There is no need to fear. We can have peace in our hearts and peace in our homes. We can be an influence for good in this world, every one of us (Gordon B. Hinckley).*[4]

- *Fear thou not; for I am with thee. . . . I will strengthen thee; yea, I will help thee (Isaiah 41:10).*

- *We need not live in fear of the future. . . . If we follow the promptings of the Spirit, we will be safe, whatever the future holds. We will be shown what to do (Boyd K. Packer).*[5]

Whatever befalls this generation, we have promises. It is our privilege to live free of fear and full of peace. With his peace in our homes, we can rise to the best standard of our race. Our mission is not to ride out the storm but to rub shoulders energetically and peaceably with mankind (D&C 45:66).

In what may have been his last letter, Mormon gave Moroni a heart-rending summary of recent horrors among their people (Moroni 9:7–19). But then he gave this advice. It is good counsel for those who are surrounded by extreme sadness:

> *My son, be faithful in Christ; and may not the things which I have written grieve thee, to weigh thee down unto death; but may Christ lift thee up, and may his sufferings and death, and the showing his body unto our fathers, and his mercy and long-suffering, and the hope of his glory and of eternal life, rest in your mind forever (Moroni 9:25).*

In a similar dark hour, the prophet Peter gave similar counsel. He concluded with a blessing upon his beloved people in these few words:

> *Peace be with you all that are in Christ Jesus (1 Peter 5:14).*

Like Christ himself, that peace is as real now as it was then. The place where it may do the most good and where it is most at home is at home.

Notes

1. In *Collected Discourses,* comp. Brian H. Stuy, 5 vols. (Salt Lake City: B. H. S. Publishing, 1987–92), 1:326.
2. Ibid., 3:392.
3. *History of The Church of Jesus Christ of Latter-day Saints,* ed. B. H. Roberts, 7 vols., 2d ed. rev. (Salt Lake City: The Church of Jesus Christ of Latter-day Saints, 1932–51), 5:98.
4. "The Times in Which We Live," *Ensign,* November 2001, 74.
5. "The Cloven Tongues of Fire," *Ensign,* May 2000, 9.

Chapter 50

THE FRIENDS OF GOD

In the mortal world we get accustomed to flaws. We learn to like each other's imperfect appearance, forgive each other's unheavenly personalities, and lock arms when one of us is weary. We take turns pushing someone else's wheelchair, as it were. Life trains us to be merciful.

When we would be disgusted or critical, God whispers, "Nay, speak no ill."[1] When we ask, "Have I done any good in the world today?"[2] he cares about the answer. He wants us not only to forgive but also to save.

> *They were set to be a light unto the world, and to be the saviors of men (D&C 103:9; 103:10; Obadiah 1:21).*

When Abraham learned that the cities of Sodom and Gomorrah were ripe for destruction, he pled for them in pity (Genesis 18:23–33), showing by his mercy that he was "the Friend of God" (James 2:23). God's friends have a drive to bless, a knack for mercy, an eye for hope. They join in the business of reclaiming what was lost (Matthew 18:11; Luke 19:10; 2 Nephi 3:24; D&C 124:28; Moses 1:39).

> *Whosoever will be great among you, shall be your minister: And whosoever of you will be the chiefest, shall be servant of all. For even the Son of man came not to be ministered unto, but to minister (Mark 10:43–45).*

When the Savior says that ministering is his sole interest, he is not just saying nice words. He is telling the truth. The Father and the Son have distinct forms and personalities, yet one way of describing them is, simply, *love* (1 John 4:8, 16). Our best response to their love is to become their partners. Like Jesus, we try to save whatever is put into our hands, and he personally appreciates the partnership (Matthew 25:21, 23, 40, 45; James 5:20; 1 John 4:11; JST, Revelation 19:10; D&C 13:1; 76:42–43; Abraham 2:12–13).

For example, Enos learned to pray for that which was lost, and then he lived a life to match his prayers (Enos 1:13–18). Looking back on this repeating cycle of unselfish prayer and saving service, he "rejoiced in it above that of the world" (Enos 1:26). Enos was like Abraham and Sarah, and there are many like him. Christ has many friends, all of them advocates for their loved ones. Their covenant is to do good in this world and to continue doing good forever (Matthew 10:39). A good system of good friends who do good, organized by the covenant, is what the Church is supposed to be (Deuteronomy 7:6–8; 2 Nephi 6:2; Mosiah 18:8–10; Alma 4:20; 43:2; 49:30; Ether 12:10). It is a realm in which, and from which, mercy flows (Matthew 6:14–15).

Justice reigns outside this sweet fellowship; mercy reigns within it. That may in some ways seem unfair, but we can be glad that a stronghold of mercy may be found somewhere in the universe of unbending law. Fairness, in its ultimate form, is justice. Who, in their mortal walk, can survive that? But inside the covenant—the fortress of mercy—fairness is softened, adjusted to the repentance of each soul. There, we can breathe instead of being choked by our sins. We can improve instead of being perpetually chained to the counter of accountability for our wrongs. Our mission is not so much to make things fair but to invite every willing person into that realm of mercy.

Lehi was one of the mercy-minded members of the covenant. Even in a dream, he was true to it, beckoning—always beckoning his family to the refreshing fruit. No doubt he is still beckoning his posterity from the other side of the veil (1 Nephi 8:15). We might say, "Of course he beckons to them. They are family." Yes, family love harmonizes precisely with this merciful order of things. Is it fair that family leaders reach out so forgivingly, so hopefully, and so patiently to their own kin? Perhaps not fair but merciful.

By the way Lehi kept the covenant, he invited Christ into his family. And then he invited his family to Christ. Nephi was just one who accepted Lehi's plea. Even this good son depended heavily on the mercy of Christ (2 Nephi 4:26, 31–32; 11:4–7). Evidently the secret of great souls is not that they possess some rare, natural greatness, for greatness sleeps in all of us. The secret, rather, is spiritual nutrition. In that special corner of the universe known as the Church of the Lamb of God grows a distinctive fruit (1 Nephi 15:36; Alma 32:40). The secret of the friends of God is that they partake of this fruit often.

> *They came forth and fell down and partook of the fruit of the tree (1 Nephi 8:30).*

When telling his family about his dream, Lehi was careful to mention this detail about falling before the tree. Before our Friend and his ample tree, we instinctively kneel. How can we stand before such fortune? Though we realize that countless others have rallied to him by covenant, we marvel to know that this is a personal matter. The fruit is personally *from* him, and it is personally *for* us. Worshiping, we taste a life-giving sweetness exceeding anything the world can grow or know. We bask in this greatest of all friendships (1 Nephi 11:21–22; Romans 5:5). Arising, we turn to our loved ones and do what Lehi did. We share with them an inviting home.

Notes

1. *Hymns of The Church of Jesus Christ of Latter-day Saints* (Salt Lake City: The Church of Jesus Christ of Latter-day Saints, 1985), no. 233.
2. Ibid., 223.

Chapter 51

Keeping Our "Possessions"

Upon mount Zion shall be deliverance, and there shall be holiness; and the house of Jacob shall possess their possessions. . . . And saviours shall come up on mount Zion (Obadiah 1:17, 21).

Why would the people of Zion have to "possess their possessions"? Because the only "possessions" worth keeping must be sealed to them so that they never lose them. The people who provide this wonderful sealing service will be "saviors," redemptive workers in the latter-day Zion. There are a lot of people to connect. Though the workers are somewhat few, the priceless "possessions" will all be sealed, one connection at a time (JST, Matthew 9:43; Jacob 5:70–71).

But a sealing ordinance is only one part of the connection. Each connection calls for a great individual effort to learn, choose, and change. Each of us comes into the covenant at our own pace—many at a snail's pace, others seemingly in reverse. To possess our possessions can be a long process.

They shall bow down under the prisoners, and they shall fall under the slain (Isaiah 10:4; 2 Nephi 20:4).

The parents of the wayward know this feeling, bowing under the weight of a "prisoner"—their own wayward child, perhaps dispirited, perhaps addicted. When Nephi saw the dark future of his own distant descendants, he could not carry the burden by himself:

I was overcome because of my afflictions, for I considered that mine afflictions were great above all (1 Nephi 15:5).

Nephi, because he had a redemptive heart, had special reasons to ache. But he also knew by experience what to do when staggering under the burden of failing loved ones. First, he received strength from the One who knows more than anyone about grief (1 Nephi 15:6). Then, with that strength, Nephi went to work so that his father Lehi and his Father in Heaven could "keep" their children. He had to get on with his mission of migration, record keeping, teaching, ship building, and nation building. He had to do his part in sharing the fruit—setting in motion as many blessings as possible for as many people as possible. To the mountainous offering of the Redeemer, he added what pebbles he could.

Our small offerings make a difference. For example, King Benjamin stood before his people, trembling "exceedingly" because of failing health, doing his best to speak clearly (Mosiah 2:30), and ardently inviting them to Christ. They needed Christ rather than Benjamin. And yet, what would have been the result if Benjamin had not given himself to this last effort? What invitation would then have been given to his people? What love-inspired response would then have welled up in their hearts? The Savior gave himself, and King Benjamin's people accepted his gift by giving themselves in return. But the teacher-leader played a small redemptive part, a part that called for giving. Giving what? Whatever it took, whatever he had. This was the way Benjamin operated, "laboring with all the might of his body and the faculty of his whole soul" (Words of Mormon 1:18).

Of course, none of this effort, be it with son or stranger, must ever be overbearing. We cannot keep our possessions forcibly. We are careful never to violate "the choice and initiative of the potential recipient" (Dallin H. Oaks).[1] It is never our mission to be bossy or dogmatic. "The least hint of unkindness acts as a circuit-breaker," tripping the flow of Christ's influence (Hugh Nibley).[2]

> *Our children are like we are; we couldn't be driven; we can't be driven now. . . . Men are not in the habit of being driven; they are not made that way (Joseph F. Smith).*[3]

So we reach out to our loved ones gently, not only because that way is right but also because there is no other way. Pressure pushes outward. It pushes people away, the opposite of keeping. It has always been so.

If we work in the Lord's patient, positive ways, we will lose no ground with the wayward dear ones. Instead, we have a promise that the Holy Ghost will be our "constant companion" in the project. We are guaranteed an "everlasting dominion" for influencing others (D&C 121:46). Christ seems to be assuring us, "Live with your loved ones in my way, speak to them in my way, react to them in my way, and I will grant your fondest dream. I will be in their midst. You will finally have them and bless them forever and ever."

If, in the short run, we do not seem to have such a dominion, if at present our touch or scepter seems to have no flame or effect, we need not despair in the least. God's calendar holds a greater resource of time than we can know. We do all the good we can, and new doors will open in time.

A good way to begin is to fill ourselves with ever more charity and virtue (D&C 121:45). We cannot have the promised influence with our loved ones if we harbor a sour outlook on our companions. The person most likely to bring another into the covenant is the one who is keeping it. The couple most likely to bring a child home is the couple with "hearts knit together in unity and in love one towards another" (Mosiah 18:21; 2 Nephi 1:21).

The voice of such a couple in prayer is heard distinctly in higher courtyards, for their pure hearts fit in so perfectly there. Their prayers resemble the concern and pleading found among heavenly members of the holy order.

> *All that we are commanded to do in this life is patterned after that of a better life. Do you think it a strange thought that maybe part of the power of family prayer is in the fact that we are part of a heavenly family, that they are interested in us, and that by tying in with them some way we get hold of something much bigger than ourselves?*
>
> *Think of the power of the thousands of prayers of parents and grandparents and back and back even to Jacob and Isaac and Abraham and beyond, all requesting essentially the same thing: "Bless my children. Bless my children. Bless my children." Can you hear it as it rolls and echoes throughout all eternity? Let us all be part of that great power for good. I testify that time and space are no barriers to these righteous influences (John H. Groberg).*[4]

If we focus a pure and powerful force upon the barrier before us, that barrier must finally move (3 Nephi 27:1). The hard part is not going through the barrier. The challenge is to gather, to join our separate powers into one power. It is the principle behind a laser beam, or the edge of a knife, or the propulsion of a jet engine: a concentration of everything on one spot.

This is just what happens when we live the gospel covenant. Heavenly forces combine with ours. When a wife and husband jointly keep the covenant, they multiply the blessings of an approving heaven and are allied with powerful friends. No matter what odds seem to favor those who seek to take away our children, they cannot match the forces that are joined under God's covenant (2 Kings 6:16; 2 Chronicles 32:7–8).

The Church is the source of untold family blessings. It is the fountainhead of the covenant, the institution that teaches the family how to be heavenly. We can be "blessed forever" in the heavenly order if we are "lively members" of the earthly order, which is the Church of Jesus Christ (D&C 92:2). The Church is the natural and ordained ally of the family. We cannot afford to turn inwardly in the name of family. To care about our own while withdrawing from the wider work of the Church is to ignore the family we have had for eons.

If we want the Father's help with our family, we should help him with his family. In both realms, we learn to work his way. In both labors, he works at our side. He has said not only that we will bring forth fruit but also that our "fruit should remain" (John 15:16). Those we bring forth will not simply be temporary joys to us, destined to pass from his arms or our arms. They will remain. If we give our service to him and find a reason to petition him concerning the particular family he has given us, he answers with this promise, "Whatsoever ye shall ask of the Father in my name, he may give it you" (John 15:16).

Notes

1. "Sharing the Gospel," *Ensign,* November 2001, 9; see also Alma 38:12.
2. *Old Testament and Related Studies* (Salt Lake City: Deseret Book, 1986), 96; see also D&C 121:37.
3. *Gospel Doctrine* (Salt Lake City: Deseret Book, 1986), 316.
4. "The Power of Family Prayer," *Ensign,* May 1982, 52; see also 3 Nephi 18:21.

Chapter 52

A Saving Family

If we have family heartaches, we are in good company. Adam and Eve had wayward children (Moses 5:27). And then there was Abraham and Sarah, who had wayward offspring *and* parents. Isaac and Rebekah had their Esau. The Prophet Joseph patiently awaits the return of his descendants to the Church for which he sacrificed everything.

If we thumb through the history of faithful people, we see an almost endless list of those who shared in the plight of family sorrow. We do not find any of these great men and women giving up—growing resentful, despondent, or unkind. While they are true to the covenant, they are tender toward the drifting soul.

As an illustration, we remember Lehi's family. Evidently, Laman and Lemuel never did taste the sweet fruit (1 Nephi 8:35). But Lehi neither gave up on Laman and Lemuel nor loved them any less for their folly and unfaithfulness. He did fear "lest they should be cast off from the presence of the Lord," but embedded in that fear was the undying hope of "a tender parent." He and Sariah could imagine that "perhaps the Lord would be merciful to them" (1 Nephi 8:36–37).

If Lehi could not tolerate the loss of Laman and Lemuel, if Sariah found it unthinkable to give up on any of her children, does it make sense for us to lose hope? No, not ever. For most families, the fulness will come in stages.

For most miracles, God uses time as the major ingredient. He uses the long run.

> *Behold, you have had many afflictions because of your family; nevertheless, I will bless you and your family, yea, your little ones; and the day cometh that they will believe and know the truth and be one with you in my church (D&C 31:2).*

God will keep his promise on his schedule. Our families will be saved by grace but only after all of our tears, prayers, family councils and outings, and family home evenings, and only after all of our service in the Church, virtuous living, patience, and good cheer (2 Nephi 25:23). Then God's hand will finish what he started (2 Nephi 27:23; Mosiah 27:14; Moroni 7:27).

In every home, the process must start with someone being true to his word (2 Nephi 30:2). The floodgates of mercy can open upon many if someone will turn the key. Every family needs a member who says, "This canoe needs at least one paddle in the water. Somebody around here had better be keeping the covenant. That will be me." Then the miracle can spread, as it did from Alma to Amulek and from Amulek to his own family (Alma 8:10, 14–20, 27; 10:7, 11).

So not only is family the end, or the grand aim, of salvation, but for many, it is also the *means* of salvation. Some people are so constituted that only a family fold can draw them into the fold of Christ. Their only path to the eternal home lies through a miniature, earthly replica of that home. Only by a living manifestation of Christ's warmth can these people be drawn to him. We all know such people. I am one of them. Very likely you are too.

When many family members are not the living testimonies they should be, just one member can have this effect, especially when the lessons of a modest life press on over every challenge, year after year. One faithful person, subsidized by the influences of heaven, is not just one at all.

> *You parents of the willful and the wayward! Don't give them up. Don't cast them off. They are not utterly lost. The Shepherd will find his sheep. They were his before they were yours—long before he entrusted them to your care; and you cannot begin to love them as he loves them. . . . Our Heavenly Father is far more merciful, infinitely more charitable, than even the best of his servants, and the Everlasting Gospel is mightier in power to save than our narrow finite minds can comprehend (Orson F. Whitney).*[1]

Inspiring as courageous mortals can be, none of them has the stunning resolve of God himself. God never gives up. His commitment is as measureless as the great universe he governs. We should notice this trait in him, we should become acquainted with this tone in his words, we should let his fire affect us, and we should try to have a more unconquerable faith of our own. Our optimism should be unvarying and sacred. We should specialize in saving.

Think of how these words from Isaiah might be likened unto "the children thou shalt have" (1 Nephi 21:20):

> *Then shalt thou say in thine heart: Who hath begotten me these, seeing I have lost my children. . . . Who hath brought up these? Behold, I was left alone; these, where have they been? (1 Nephi 21:21; 19:24).*

Some of those unexpected sons and daughters will be new to us, a wondrous harvest from generations yet unborn. But others will be the very ones we raised and may have thought we lost, supposing they would never come back.

The slow, permanent math of the covenant provides a route of return, even for those who have been gone a long time. The return may come after losses and sorrows. It may be more difficult than words can say. The lost "child" of promise may be a young adult, aged, or even deep into post-mortal life before turning homeward. But the prospect of a return is still in place. It is as real as the covenant itself (Proverbs 22:6; 2 Nephi 4:5).

> *Though some of the sheep may wander, the eye of the Shepherd is upon them, and sooner or later they will feel the tentacles of Divine Providence reaching out after them and drawing them back to the fold. Either in this life or the life to come, they will return (Orson F. Whitney).*[2]

They are not drawn back against their will. But the "tentacles"—the powerful arms of attraction and affection—have a long and patient reach. Those tentacles are inherent in the mega-generation family we will find in the spirit world. That vastly larger family is an active one and a saving one.

> *Neither have angels ceased to minister unto the children of men. . . . And the office of their ministry is to call men unto repentance, and to fulfil and to do the work of the covenants of the Father. . . . And after this manner bringeth to pass the Father, the covenants which he hath made unto the children of men (Moroni 7:29, 31–32).*

Despite appearances, the saving family is the one lasting fixture. Eventually, despite temporary allegiances along the way, the bills are sent to the home address. It is the right of family to pay, to save, to be there permanently for the lost or slipping soul, to make the modest, repeated efforts that count the most and that last the longest. It is the right of family to pray and love and hope and save forever.

> *Pray for your careless and disobedient children; hold on to them with your faith. Hope on, trust on, till you see the salvation of God (Orson F. Whitney).*[3]

Notes

1. In Conference Reports of The Church of Jesus Christ of Latter-day Saints (Salt Lake City: The Church of Jesus Christ of Latter-day Saints, April 1929), 110.
2. Ibid.
3. Ibid.

Chapter 53

A Saving Covenant

Verily, thus saith the Lord unto you, my friends Sidney and Joseph, your families are well; they are in mine hands, and I will do with them as seemeth me good; for in me there is all power (D&C 100:1).

Sidney and Joseph had been away and were worried about things at home. They had no way to get in touch and no speedy way to return. The only thing going for them was that they were trying very hard to serve the Lord.

Even though we are at home, there may still be giant gaps we cannot fill. But this one thing we can always do: keep our obligations to God so that according to his promises he can watch over those gaps day and night (1 Nephi 14:14; 21:25; 2 Nephi 6:17; Mosiah 29:20; D&C 45; 121:33–37).

The mighty God shall deliver his covenant people. For thus saith the Lord, I will contend with them that contend with thee, and I will save thy children (JST, Isaiah 49:25).

Does the insidious adversary himself contend with you over a loved one? Does it seem that you are losing your child to the dark, old kidnapper of human history? The mighty God promises family salvation (2 Nephi 7–9; Isaiah 54:10).

Of course, one person is not excused from righteousness because another person keeps the covenant. But if the Savior could speak to our wayward loved ones, he might say this:

> *The Father having . . . sent me to bless you in turning away every one of you from his iniquities; and this because ye are the children of the covenant (3 Nephi 20:26; D&C 62:1).*

Through our faithfulness, others can be repeatedly invited and humbled until they finally want to repent. If we keep the covenant with all our hearts, our loved ones will someday see the need to come unto Christ with all their hearts. They will do so sincerely, for turning to Christ insincerely is not turning to him at all. If we have trouble inviting a child into the kingdom, we can enthusiastically build up that kingdom in the meantime (Deuteronomy 7:12). If we labor in the Lord's harvest, we will in due time gather our own sheaves (Alma 26:5–8).

> *When a seal is put upon the father and mother, it secures their posterity, so that they cannot be lost, but will be saved by virtue of the covenant of the father and mother (Joseph Smith).*[1]

When the ordinance is performed and the covenant is kept by the father and mother, it is eventually sealed upon them. Then the providences of God are unleashed—the long, sensitive, and yet awesome forces of the covenant may then go their length. Here is Brigham Young's restatement of this promise:

> *Let the father and mother . . . take a righteous course, and strive with all their might never to do a wrong, but to do good all their lives; if they have one child or one hundred children, if they conduct themselves towards them as they should, binding them to the Lord by their faith and prayers,*

I care not where those children go, they are bound up to their parents by an everlasting tie, and no power of earth or hell can separate them from their parents in eternity; they will return again to the fountain from whence they sprang (Brigham Young).[2]

The gospel covenant is designed not only to seal families but also to heal them. It wipes away tears, closes wounds, and draws prodigal sons and daughters back home. But the covenant blesses most where it is kept the best. Most of us could do a better job of honoring it, bringing our best Family Friend into the home and invoking the blessings of the Atonement upon the painful spots in our families.

Covenants remembered by parents will be remembered by God. The children may thus become the beneficiaries and inheritors of these great covenants and promises. This is because they are the children of the covenant (James E. Faust).[3]

If we feel our backs against the wall, if the lifestyle of someone precious to us is wrenching our hearts by day and robbing our sleep by night, we can trust the covenant in two ways. First, for our happiness, for our child, and for that child's Heavenly Parent, we can keep the terms of the covenant with all our hearts as a lasting act of faith.

When parents keep the covenants they have made at the altar of the temple, their children will be forever bound to them (Boyd K. Packer).[4]

Second, we can trust so calmly in the God of promises that we do not worry. We can have his peace. We can let his cheer and reassurance brighten our conversations and emotions. We can be full of hope. We can then be free in our hearts to notice some good things.

We will notice good things about our imperfect family members. We will notice the good cheer of the promises and the good destiny that awaits us. We will notice that the Family Friend we have invited into our homes is watching and slowly influencing our families. We will receive the good tidings and rejoice in the blessings that God and his prophets have pronounced upon us.

> *May there be . . . a sense of security and peace and love among your children, precious children every one of them, even those who may have strayed. I hope you don't lose patience with them; I hope you go on praying for them, and I don't hesitate to promise that if you do so, the Lord will touch their hearts and bring them back to you with love and respect and appreciation (Gordon B. Hinckley).*[5]

Notes

1. *Teachings of the Prophet Joseph Smith*, sel. Joseph Fielding Smith (Salt Lake City: Deseret Book, 1976), 321.
2. In *Journal of Discourses*, 26 vols. (London: Latter-day Saints' Book Depot, 1854–86), 11:215.
3. "The Greatest Challenge in the World—Good Parenting," *Ensign*, November 1990, 35.
4. "Our Moral Environment," *Ensign*, May 1992, 68.
5. "Prophet Returns to 'Beloved England,'" *Church News*, 2 September 1995, 4.

Chapter 54

He Will Not Barge In

Mine eyes are upon you, and the heavens and the earth are in mine hands, and the riches of eternity are mine to give (D&C 67:2).

It is not enough to know that our Father possesses all the wealth of the universe. His *purpose* is what tells us most about him, and that purpose is "to give" those riches. His holdings and powers are not for personal hoarding or indulgence. He is in the business of sharing.

None is acceptable before God, save the meek and lowly in heart (Moroni 7:44).

My grace is sufficient for the meek (Ether 12:26).

He would prefer to bestow everything on every one of us, but that depends on whether we are meek. By inheriting the earth and its destiny, the meek inherit the celestial kingdom (Psalm 37:11; Matthew 5:5; 3 Nephi 12:5; D&C 38:17–20; 88:17–20). That is, they inherit all things (D&C 76:50–70).

The meek receive all that God has because they are willing to do all that he asks (JST, Genesis 14:31; Philippians 4:13; D&C 101:60, 62; 123:17; Abraham 3:25–26). This is their strength, the might of total devotion. It is not obedience to just anyone, not a servile tendency to please whoever comes along. The meekness that leads to exaltation is specifically and personally focused upon the one right Master.

Teach them to never be weary of good works, but to be meek and lowly in heart (Alma 37:34).

God grants his riches to his reliable children—those who do not quit on him or grow weary (Helaman 10:4–5). How could he give unlimited riches to one who has limited humility, limited integrity, limited generosity, limited virtue? Meekness is the perfect trait for wielding perfect power (Numbers 12:3). The more we understand this trait, the more we will understand Jesus. It was the reason for his flawless record on earth. Meekness is the center of his character (Matthew 11:29; 3 Nephi 27:13; D&C 20:22). The perfect school for this perfect trait is the gospel covenant.

Keeping the covenant is the process for inheriting all that our Father has, and meekness is the principle behind that process. We can become the Father's genuine heirs only if we live as his genuine children.

In meekness before the Lord we always remember him. In meekness we are chaste, honest, and benevolent. The husband meekly gives himself to the roles of providing, protecting, and presiding, and by that very same virtue his angel companion nurtures, beautifies, and sweetens the life of their home. By meekness we invite the nobles of heaven—our offspring—to be our houseguests, and then we live together with them in grace and order. In the strength of meekness, we accept the mission of helping them with their growth and salvation, no matter what their weaknesses.

Our meekness is a pleasant offering—pleasant to God and to us (1 Peter 3:4). It is an offering in the similitude of the meek and lowly Jesus (Moses 5:7). As animals of sacrifice were subdued and placed upon altars in days of old, so with our hearts now. As surely as the smoke rose from those sacrifices, so the prayers we offer in our sacrifices are guaranteed to rise and be "a sweet savour" to God (Exodus 29:18; 2 Corinthians 2:15).

> *Behold, I stand at the door, and knock: if any man hear my voice, and open the door, I will come in to him, and will sup with him, and he with me (Revelation 3:20).*

At what other doors, except the doors of our homes, would he knock? He has the keys to everything else. He may come and go as he pleases anywhere in the galaxies except into shut-off souls or shouting homes (Matthew 23:28–29). He is a gentleman. Because of his perfect meekness, he will not come barging in to redeem and save. We must open the door, receive, welcome. By our meekness we invite him in.

Chapter 55

A Kingdom Is Prepared

He that goeth forth and weepeth, bearing precious seed, shall doubtless come again with rejoicing, bringing his sheaves with him (Psalm 126:6).

We cannot imagine that day of relief and rejoicing (Isaiah 64:4; D&C 133:45). We cannot, for joy thereof, grasp what it will be to return home, bringing our family members—the sheaves of our harvest—with us (Isaiah 51:3; Zechariah 2:10–13; Zephaniah 3:14–17).

But before long, we will have a preview. The coming of Christ will be a celebration of family blessings, showing that earthly parents can be made into eternal ones. His advent will be the beginning of great days for the pure in heart. The ancient promises to fathers and mothers will begin to be fulfilled (JST, Genesis 9:21; Deuteronomy 7:9; Matthew 5:8; D&C 97:21; 109:75–76; Moses 7:63; relating to the meeting at Adam-ondi-Ahman, which will be conducted by our father Adam, see Daniel 7:13–14, 22 and D&C 78:15–16).

They that remain, and are pure in heart, shall return, and come to their inheritances, they and their children, with songs of everlasting joy, to build up the waste places of Zion (D&C 101:18).

So far we know the inheritance in small part. What will be its fulness? What will it be to know that fulness forever? What will it mean to have the full inheritance of God not only forever but also *together?*

Eternal life means to live forever in exalted spheres in companionship with those we cherish, encompassed about by profound love, exquisite joy, and glory. No amount of money can purchase this exalted state (Joseph B. Wirthlin).[1]

Inheriting God's kingdom is not merely gaining the right to enter and enjoy a nice view. Imagine being told that you had inherited a watch but were not allowed to wear it, or that someone had given you a palace but that you could only visit the entrance for a few minutes each day before having to leave. What sort of inheritance is that? Such a "gift" makes a mockery of giving. To be a full heir is to receive entire access, to govern the inheritance, to own in full.

Our inheritance is more than a place, more than possessions. We acquire from God his virtues, his powers, and his kind of relationships. Just as his family life forever expands, we too will have the privilege of increase (D&C 131:4; 132:19–20, 23–24).

Those who are married by the power and authority of the priesthood in this life, and continue without committing the sin against the Holy Ghost, will continue to increase and have children in the celestial glory (Joseph Smith).[2]

This exaltation is already on the calendar, and our "kingdoms" are already prepared (D&C 98:18). And yet, we still have work to do—helping the Father extend his kingdom before we enter our own and helping him fulfill his covenant in other families besides our own. In meekness we will find the burden light, the labor sweet (Matthew 11:29–30). The work of the covenant will polish us for our destiny. When that work is complete and when we are complete, we will hear the gentle voice welcome us in

(Matthew 25:34; Joshua 21:45; Isaiah 54:10–17; 2 Nephi 9:18; Ether 4:19; D&C 64:30–32; 76:3).

> *The foxes have holes, and the birds of the air have nests; but the Son of man hath not where to lay his head (Matthew 8:20).*

Small animals can sneak in wherever they choose to find rest. But the Son of Man, heir to all the earth and its dwellings and comforts, awaits an invitation. His mind is full of wise ways to bless everyone in the covenant home. Managing all the hosts of heaven and earth, he longs to help us manage, for we cannot manage without him. It is not the gloom outside our homes that he seeks most to dispel but the gloom within. To give him a place in our sitting room, to let him sup with us, and to offer a soft place for his precious head is a simple matter.

> *No ear may hear his coming;*
> *But in this world of sin,*
> *Where meek souls will receive him, still*
> *The dear Christ enters in.*[3]

Christ is drawn to certain homes. He enters easily where promises are kept. Fortunately, he is acquainted with our weaknesses. He understands that we are only slightly acquainted with him. He copes calmly with our sluggish reactions. He invites us to his meetings and to his temple. In perfect hospitality, he provides a place for us to lay down our burdens, to rest our heads. He schedules times and raises up friends here and there to relieve our bloated stress. He lets us persist a while in focusing on ourselves, he waits and waits until we wake up and answer his patient knocking at our door. He looks forward to the time when we ask what *he* wants (Helaman 10:4–5).

That is when the greater blessings of Christ will abide in our families. Then, by the Father's wonderful covenant, we will host the Lord of hosts himself.

The darkness of the world, I fear,
Would in my home abide.
O Savior, stay this night with me;
Behold, 'tis eventide.[4]

Our Old Testament friends renewed their invitations to the Lord by the sacrifices that burned with holy fire upon stone altars. Since then, he has ordained another way, which we call the sacrament of the Lord's Supper. The offering is within, and the holy fire responds to it within. But the invitation is still official and real.

While on their way to Emmaus, Cleopas and his companion asked the resurrected Jesus to abide with them. Later, as they sat to eat, he broke bread and gave it to them. He vanished from their sight when they recognized him, but he stayed on with them through the burning within their hearts (Luke 24:13–32). That was a blessed home! But our homes might be just that blessed through the same invitation. At the ordained time each week, we may bestir ourselves and answer his knock. By remembering his offering represented through the bread and water and by renewing the offering of our vows to him, we invite our Friend to spend yet another week in our homes.

After a thousand such weeks—or ten thousand such weeks—he will look on his right hand and find your family, whole and grateful, gathered there. Smiling upon all of you, he will speak this invitation:

> *Come, ye blessed of my Father, inherit the kingdom prepared for you from the foundation of the world (Matthew 25:34).*

As surely as we invite him to join us in earthy homes and imperfect families today, in due time he will invite *us* to join him in a place that he has already prepared (John 14:2–3; D&C 98:18).

Notes

1. "Follow Me," *Ensign,* May 2002, 16.
2. *Teachings of the Prophet Joseph Smith,* sel. Joseph Fielding Smith (Salt Lake City: Deseret Book, 1976), 301.
3. *Hymns of The Church of Jesus Christ of Latter-day Saints* (Salt Lake City: The Church of Jesus Christ of Latter-day Saints, 1985), no. 208.
4. Ibid., 165.

Chapter 56

GLIMPSES

THE PRAYER OF THE RIGHTEOUS

Let us suppose that two people of the covenant are deeply concerned about some struggling family member. Each makes the loved one a subject of prayer, but while one prays only for this single family member, the other approaches God in behalf of many others in need besides the immediate loved one.

Though each of these persons has about the same amount of discretionary money, one pays a full tithe and gives generous fast offerings while the other does not. Though each has about the same amount of discretionary time, only one serves diligently in Church assignments and attends meetings faithfully. The other attends meetings only occasionally and prefers not to have any Church callings. One studies the scriptures daily; the other reads them now and then if a big need arises.

As we all know, faithfulness varies among those who plead with the Lord to bless their families and marriages. Every prayer is heard because those who pray have some kind of faith or they would offer no prayer at all. God will answer their prayers and exercise mercy in his wisdom.

But the question still remains: Will there be a different kind of mercy for one than the other? Is not this the purpose of the covenant, to open the gates of mercy more fully to those who keep their promises with all their hearts? Is there not a fulness of faith on our part that prompts a fulness of grace on God's part?

If you were wayward or out of touch with the heavens and if you desperately needed someone else's prayers, which of the two people cited above would you want to be praying for you night and day?

> *The effectual prayer of a righteous man availeth much (James 5:16; Ether 1:35–40; Enos 1:15–18).*

I WANTED THIS FEELING FOR GOOD

The following is a Christmas letter written by a young woman we will call Rachelle and addressed to her close relatives and friends. She wrote it a couple of years after going through a "mighty change." Her turning point came after many months of prayer and fasting on the part of her parents.

> I want to share with you something about our Redeemer, Jesus Christ. I don't share it lightly. It is taken from the story of my own life.
>
> From the day I was born I have had an intense curiosity for anything new. As a child I got in trouble many times and worried my parents with my "adventures." My curiosity grew as I got older, but my dedication to the gospel did not.
>
> As I reached the last two years of junior high, I was praying less, reading my scriptures less and less, until finally I didn't do either. My desire to do good was leaving to make room for the wrong kinds of people, music, etc.
>
> I chose to ignore what was happening to me, but I'm sure

that you and other close friends could see. I look at old pictures of myself and wonder how I could have ever been that person.

In my tenth grade year, I pushed away the Spirit until it was no longer there. My family often spoke words of love and encouragement to me. But when I noticed that this was softening my heart, I would push it away again.

With summer came our stake girls camp. I had no intention of going, but instead of trying to get out of it, I decided to just stand it for a few days. I was even persuaded to go a day early to help make preparations. The next day, as the other girls began to arrive, I noticed how different they were from the friends I was used to. They were happy and it was sincere. This made me feel good.

There was no worldly music or immodest dress. Not even any boys. The activities were wholesome and fun at the same time. We were in the mountains, surrounded by the innocence of nature. It was a perfect place to feel the Spirit of the Lord even if you weren't looking for it.

In one of our evening gatherings, the topic was purity. The teacher asked us to share experiences when we decided to be pure. Various girls stood up and told of times when they turned off a bad show, said "no" to an alcoholic drink, or just stood up for something they knew was right. As I listened, I struggled to think of times when I had done that. But I could not. I became very distraught about this. I started to cry and was not sure why. At the time, I didn't understand that the Spirit was working on me. I tried to fight it off because I didn't want to change.

As I thought back on my old ways, a very clear thought pressed into my heart. It simply was: "Did you know that this hurts my feelings?" I knew exactly who was saying this to me. It was as if everything around me went on pause and the only thing I knew was that my Savior was extremely close to me. I could feel his presence. It overwhelmed me with such sweet and compelling love that I could not speak.

What he had said to me meant that he is real. And if that was true, the Atonement really did take place and he was resurrected. It also meant he knows all things. He was aware of me as an individual. Because this was all true, his whole gospel was true and his Church was true.

At this point, I had a choice to accept or reject this striking knowledge. I could only think about how much my Redeemer loved me. In spite of all the times I had pushed him away and ignored him, he still wanted me, Rachelle. I realized then how much I needed him and how much he wanted me to live with him once again. I decided I was going to keep this feeling. I wanted it with me for good.

At first I was scared to go to my bishop. I didn't quite understand the Atonement or the repentance process. The fear went away as I kept meeting with him. The change wrought in my heart was obvious to others and myself. Often people at work or church or school would ask what was different about me. I never did say much because inquiring meant they already knew the answer. It was hard, but I felt my Savior with me the whole way. He approved of my decision and that made it all worth it.

I had done many things to earn his disapproval, but he still wanted me. He loved me through it all. I cannot tell you all the blessings I have received since that time. One is that I only vaguely remember those terrible years of rebellion. I do remember that I had a very poor perspective. I never doubted the common sense of the gospel, but now my heart is involved. My heart changed in a matter of minutes, and now my whole life is changing.

The Atonement is very real and incredibly sweet. I have been able to attend the temple because of it. I have a testimony burning in me. It echoes back whenever I spend time with you and others who live the gospel. What my Savior did for me he will surely do for others as soon as they let him.

INDEX

A

Abraham, 51, 188, 218–19
Abraham and Sarah: as exalted couple, 38, 43–45, 104; wayward children of, 227
Adam and Eve: offering of, 35–37; as exalted couple, 38, 42–43, 72; loyalty of, 75; as meet for each other, 79, 82, 104; decision making of, 94; gentle traits of, 109; as parents, 115, 116, 227; are commanded to teach, 156–57
Administering, 182
Adoption, 116
Altars, 5, 26, 35–37
Angels, 151
Anger, 149–51
Apostasy, 81
Ashton, Marvin J., 26, 189–90
Atonement: as enveloping robe, 19–20; as gospel offering of Christ, 22, 26, 40–41, 176; fathers as proxy examples of, 107; as grace of Christ, 148, 247–48
Attraction, pure, 65

B

Ballard, Melvin J., 119
Beauty, 103–4
Benjamin, King, 223
Benson, Ezra Taft, 38
Blessing, 88, 171–73
Blessings of the fathers, 38–41
Body, physical, 202
Book of Mormon, 29, 48–49
Book of remembrance, 182–83
Brickey, Joseph, 61
Burdens, bearing each other's, 146–48

C

Cannon, George Q., 27, 191–92
Character, building, 121–24, 131–33
Chariots of Fire, 118–19
Charity, 66, 76, 144
Chastity, 65–68
Children: can strengthen marriages, 102; divinity of, 111–13, 131–32; welcoming, into world, 114–16; mighty spirits among, 117–19; helping, to gain character, 121–24, 131–33; redeeming wayward, 222–26, 227–31, 232–35, 245–48
Chores, 199–200. *See also* Work
Church of Jesus Christ of Latter-day Saints, The: as support system for family, 10–12, 226; as example of preparation, 178; as tool to build faith, 181

Civility, 76, 144–45
Clark, J. Reuben, Jr., 86
Cleopas, 61–62, 242
Clutter, 205–9
Communication, 80–81, 189–92
Comparisons, 142–43, 147
Contention, 149–51
Councils, family, 93–94, 189–92
Courtesy, 108, 144–45
Covenant couples. *See* Marriage, celestial.
Covenant, gospel: invites Christ into lives, 4, 212, 239–43; as bond of loyalty, 22–25, 27; reminders of, 28–29; celestial marriage as highest, 38, 42–45; restoration of, 39–40, 56–58; marital intimacy within, 65–68; learning of Christ through, 162–63; covenant home reflects, of Christ, 165–66, 202–4; mercy within, 219–20, 244–45; heals and seals families, 234; teaches meekness, 237
Covenant people: meaning of, 46–49; scattering of, 53–55; lack of contention among, 149; reflect culture of heaven, 152–55; as rescuers and examples, 164–66; prosper through work, 195; need not fear, 204, 214–16; as friends of God, 218–20; combine forces with heaven, 225–26, 228–31; promises to, 232–35
Creation, 81
Criticism, 141–44
Culture of heaven, 152–55

D

Debt, 206
Decision making, 81, 93–94, 121–22
Divorce, 76–78, 95–99
Dominion, unrighteous, 93–94
Dream, story of, 131–33
Driving, example of, 144

E

Earth, 70
Edification, 81
Enos, 219
Eternal increase, 240
Eternal life, 123, 239–40
Eyring, Henry B., 158

F

Facsimiles of book of Abraham, 44–45
Faith, 181–84, 195
Faithfulness, 244–45
Family: healing, through Christ, 4–5; as great constant, 6; as great plan of life, 7–9; as pearl of great price, 10–12; supported by the Church, 10–12, 226; Christ redeems and saves, 14–16; gospel offerings within, 30–32; being part of covenant, 47–48, 164–66; gathers together in Christ, 52, 58; can be scattered, 54–55; councils, 93–94, 189–92; showing grace within, 142–44, 146–48; can reflect culture of heaven, 152–55; mission, 154–55; works and plays together, 169–71, 194, 199–200; spending time with, 180; records, 182–83; showing mercy to, 219–20; promises to, 224; as means to salvation, 228–31, 232–35;

meekness within, 237. *See also* Marriage, celestial; Parenting
"Family–A Proclamation to the World, The," 58, 84, 165
Family home evenings, 159, 160
Fasting, 172
Fathers, 8, 92, 93, 107–10, 178. *See also* Parenting
Faultfinding, 129, 141–43, 147
Faust, James E., 88, 234
Fear, 204, 213–16
Fidelity, 26–29, 76
Filtering, 205
First Presidency: on sons and daughters of God, 6; on spirit of man, 6; on roles in marriage, 81–82; on womanhood, 84; on special spirits, 117
Forgiveness, 148
Friends of God, 218–20
Friendship, 144–45

G

Gabriel (Noah), 60–61
Gathering, 50–52
God the Father: as eternal parent, 6–7, 229; passes through second estate, 7; offers plan of happiness, 22, 26; trustworthiness of, 27–29; work of, 39; friends of, 218–20. *See also* Jesus Christ
Good cheer, story of, 167–68
Grace: 141–45, 146–48; and atonement of Jesus Christ, 247–48
Groberg, John H., 225

H

Happiness, great plan of: intended for families, 7–8, 10; as gospel offering of the Father, 22, 26
Harmony, 177–80, 192
Haun's Mill, 187
Hinckley, Gordon B.: on families bound together, 57; on loyalty in marriage, 74; on virtuous women, 85; on unrighteous husbands, 109; on happy parenthood, 114; on youth of today, 117; on correcting children, 129–30; on teaching gospel to family, 160; on unity in marriage, 190; on hard work, 193–94; on peace, 215; on wayward children, 235
Holy Ghost, 79–80, 83, 191
Homes: husbands preside in, 92–94, 104–5; putting, in order, 177–80, 205–9; law of, 202–4. *See also* Family
Humility, 80, 88
Hunter, Howard W., 17–18, 68, 93
Husbands: role of, 81–83, 107–10; preside in home, 92–94, 104–5

I

Inheritance, 240
Inspiration, 172–73, 191, 195
Intimacy, sexual, 65–68
Inviting Him In, 61–62
Isaac and Rebekah, 38, 75, 227
Israel, children of, 47–48, 54–57, 154

J

Jacob and Rachel, 38
Jesus Christ: seeks to be part of our lives, 3–5, 241–43; as Redeemer and Savior of families, 13–16, 212, 233, 238; as friend of families, 17–21, 61–62, 234–35; blood of, 41; as gathering center, 52; as messenger of the covenant, 57–58; prophecies of, 60–61; as healer of marriages, 75–76; heals hardened hearts, 77–78; resists Satan's temptations, 89; influence and example of, 92–93; needs example of father, 108; as example of grace, 141–44, 148; teaching about, 161–63; as Prince of Peace, 213–16; in partnership with, 218–20; meekness of, 237
Justice, 219

K

Kafar, 19, 144, 204
Kimball, Heber C., 103
Kimball, Spencer W.: on family, 8, 166; on pre-earth covenants, 47; on character development, 121; on marriage, 199
Kipper, 19–20

L

Larsen, Dean L., 117
Larsen, Sharon G., 128
Last days, 117–19
Law, of the gospel, 24
Leadership, 92–94, 103–5, 189–92
Lee, Harold B., 45
Lehi, 157, 220, 227
Light, 140
Listening, 129
Little, Eric, 118–19
"Living Christ, The," 58
Lot, 51–52
Loyalty, 74–75

M

Man, 88–91, 107–10
Manipulation, 80
Marriage, celestial: essential to great plan of happiness, 7–8; as crowning ordinance, 38, 69–73; of Adam and Eve, 42–43; of Abraham and Sarai, 43–45; purity and fidelity in, 65–68; potential of, 74–78; true companionship in, 79–83; partnership within, 92–94, 103–5; parenting within, 102, 224–25; showing grace within, 141–45, 146–48, 149–51; creation of, from covenant couple, 183–84; counciling in, 191–92
Materialism, 51–52
Maxwell, Neal A., 12, 152
McConkie, Bruce R.: on Church and family, 11; on celestial marriage, 38; on Israel, 47; on eternal life, 152
McKay, David O., 67, 90
Meekness, 236–37
Meet, for each other, 79–83
Mercy, 219–20
Ministering, 182, 218
Mission, family, 154–55

Missionaries, 178
Missionary couple, story of, 208–9
Monson, Thomas S., 196
Mormon Tabernacle Choir, 178
Moroni, 107–8
Mothers: support priesthood, 103–5; heroism and humility of, 114–16; great examples of, 134–37
Mourning, 146

N

Nadauld, Margaret D., 85
Nauvoo, trip to, 99–100
Nelson, Russell M., 84, 104, 165
Nephi, 156, 220
Nephites, 214
Nibley, Hugh, 224
Noah (Gabriel), 60–61

O

Oaks, Dallin H., 8, 224
Offerings, gospel: of God, Christ, man, 22, 26, 56; examples of, 30–32, 223; at altars, 35–37
Order, 177–80, 205–8
Ordinances, 24, 162

P

Packer, Boyd K.: on plan of happiness, 7; on sacredness of home and family, 11; on Satan's opposition, 18; on power of sexual intimacy, 67; on teaching gospel to children, 160; on good things, 195; on not fearing, 216; on children of the covenant, 234
Parenting: as essential to great plan of happiness, 8; influencing children through, 111–13, 118–19; with joy, 114–16; during teenage years, 121–25; with righteousness, 126–30; with grace, 146–48; teaching as part of, 156–59; teaching of Christ in, 160–63; in setting house in order, 177–80; gospel tools in, 181–84
Parents, heavenly, 6
Peace, 213–16
Pearl of great price, 10–12
Perfection, 3
Perry, L. Tom, 189
Peterson, Mark E., 66
Prayer: of Adam and Eve, 5; in parenting, 127–28, 225; examples of, 171–73, 244–45; for wisdom and order, 178; for spiritual health, 185
Pre-earth existence, 6–7, 132
Preparation, 121–24, 178
Priesthood: 88–94; support of, by mothers, 103–5
Priorities, 199–200
Prodigal son, 144–45
Progression, 69–70
Prophets, 187
Prosperity, 51
Public life, 153
Purity, 65–68, 90

Q

Quorum of the Twelve Apostles: on fatherhood, 8, 92, 93, 110, 178

R

Rebekah , 115. *See also* Isaac and Rebekah
Redeemer, 13–14, 143. *See also* Jesus Christ
Redemption, 222–26, 227–31
Reproving, 129
Respect, 108
Restoration, 39–41, 56–59, 99–100
Richards, Stephen L, 10
Rigdon, Sidney, 232
Robe, 19, 144, 187, 204
Roberts, B. H., 84
Roles, marriage, 80–83

S

Sabbath, 185–86
Sacrament, 26, 91, 242
Salvation, family, 15, 228–31, 232
Salvation, plan of. *See* Happiness, great plan of
Satan: seeks to destroy families, 18, 81, 164–65; tempts with sexual intimacy, 67–68; tempts Christ, 89; degrades women, 100; tempts women, 105; tempts valiant youth, 117; tactics of, 141–42, 149–51
Savior, 14–15. *See also* Jesus Christ
Saviors on Mount Zion, 222–26, 228–31
Scattering, 53–58
Scott, Richard G., 19, 67, 94
Scriptures, 157, 160–61
Sealing ordinances, 222
Sealing power, 116
Second Coming, 20, 239
Sinai, 51
Single life, 72
Smiling, story of, 167–68
Smith, Emma, 85–86
Smith, Joseph: on gathering of families, 38–39; on God gathering his people, 51, 52; on Noah as Gabriel, 60; on Adam, 79; in translating Book of Mormon, 85–86; on man's potential, 90; on eternal life, 123, 240; as a youth, 123–24; on helping others forsake sin, 143–44; prayers of, 186; on Abraham, 188; on councils, 190; on seeking peace, 215; wayward descendants of, 227, 233; family of, 232
Smith, Joseph F.: on vision of spirit world, 48; on marriage relationship, 68, 71; on correcting children with love, 147–48, 224
Smith, Lucy Mack, 187
Smoot, Reed, 116
Spirit, 202–4
Spirit, evil, story of, 17
Spiritual health, 185–88
Spouses, 79–83
Stewardship, 107–10
Stress, 205–9

T

Talmage, James E., 89, 214
Teaching: in parenting, 156–59; about Christ, 160–63

Temples, 26, 152
Time, 180, 228
Tools, faith-building, 181–84
Trust, 26–29

W

Weaknesses, 142–43
Wells, Daniel H., 7
Whitmer, David, 186
Whitney, Orson F., 229, 230, 231
Wirthlin, Joseph B., 240
Wives, 82–83, 103–5
Women, 84–86, 99–100
Woodruff, Abraham O., 195
Woodruff, Wilford, 117
Work of the Father, 39
Work, 169–71, 195–96, 199–200

Y

Young, Brigham: on marriage, 70–71; on mothers of nations, 102; on becoming Gods, 126; on living as angels, 148; on saving wayward children, 234
Youth: valiancy of, 117–19; character development of, 121–24; growth of, 126–29

Z

Zacharias, 60–61
Zion, 10, 149, 157–58